WHEN HIPPO WAS HAIRY

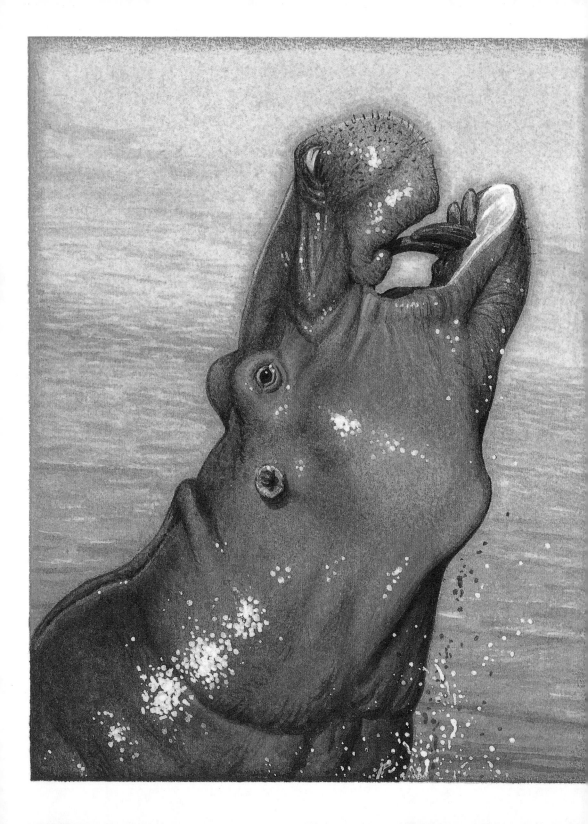

WHEN HIPPO WAS HAIRY

And other Tales from AFRICA

Told by Nick Greaves
Illustrated by Rod Clement

Bok Books International

Dedicated to my father, Roland.

Southern African edition.
This edition co-published in South Africa by
Bok Books International, Mbabane, Swaziland
and Durban, R.S.A.
ISBN 0 947444-11-4 (hard cover)
ISBN 0 947444-12-2 (paperback)

First published hard cover 1988
First published paperback 1989
Reprinted 1990, 1991, 1992, 1993

A David Bateman Book
Typeset by Typeset Graphics Ltd.
Printed in Hong Kong by Everbest Printing Co.
Designed by Errol McLeary

Contents

Acknowledgements

A great many people helped in the preparation of this book — some knowingly, some unwittingly. For their advice and for additional information I am indebted to: Dr. John Hutton, former Curator of Mammology, and Dr. Don Broadley, Curator of Herpetology, both of the Natural History Museum of Zimbabwe; Mr. Ron Thomson, former Provincial Warden, Hwange National Park; Mr. Ian Thomson, former Warden, Matopos National Park; Mr. Ivan Ncube, Provincial Warden, Matabeleland South; Mr. Mike Jones, Terrestrial Ecologist, Hwange National Park, Zimbabwe Department of National Parks and Wildlife Management; Dr. Rosalie Osbourne of the Kenya Wildlife Conservation and Management Department; Mr. Francis Odoom and the Languages Institute of Ghana. Special thanks are also due to Bookie and Rich Peek and Mr. Hadebe, Chief Librarian, the Natural History Museum of Zimbabwe.

A great deal of technical information and support came from Kodak USA and Canon Inc. of Japan. The photographs, I hope, were of assistance to the illustrator, Mr. Rod Clement.

Most of all I am indebted to my typist, associate editor, and to my son, Douglas, for being a patient "sounding board."

Introduction

Until quite recently the African continent possessed not only the greatest concentration of wild animals in the world, but the greatest variety too. Sadly, those almost endless herds are now a thing of the past.

The interior of Africa was a place of mystery to all but a handful of adventurous (and often foolhardy) explorers, hunters and missionaries, until the early 1900s. The memoirs of men like Thomas Baines, David Livingstone, P. Courtney Selous and Jonathan Speake, tell us how rich and bountiful was the wildlife of such areas as the East African Plateau and the Karoo.

However, among them, the "gentlemen hunters," the Voortrekkers, the ivory hunters and eventually the farmers, started a slaughter so complete that in many areas of Africa the indigenous animals were exterminated.

Luckily, people have now come to recognize the richness and beauty of the few remaining wilderness areas, and much is being done to conserve them. The benefits of conservation are both financial and aesthetic — but it is future generations who pose the greatest threat to the remaining wildlife.

As Africa's population explodes at an alarming rate, people will require more food and therefore more land, which is a limited resource. Already game parks and sanctuaries are being eyed with envy by land-hungry people. Let us hope that we can develop the future without the destruction that has typified Africa's development in the past.

One of the legacies of Africa's erstwhile teeming wildlife is the wealth of folklore and mythology surrounding it. Indeed, the richness of the lore mirrors the richness of the wildlife. Many of the tales, although told by different tribes from region to region, are basically similar, and they remain a source of knowledge and enjoyment to us and to future generations.

This book attempts to illustrate to our ever-expanding urban population not only the folklore and mythology, but some of the more interesting facts about various animals of the African bush.

The tales of old need not be a thing of the past; the wildlife which inspired them, brought endearingly alive by these simple stories, is a part of Africa's heritage which should not be forgotten.

General Information

DISTRIBUTION (See maps)

The various animals highlighted in this book are all found in southern Africa, though some are also widely spread throughout the rest of sub-Saharan Africa. It is interesting that some species restricted to southern Africa, such as the tsessebe, rock dassie and chacma baboon, do have very close relatives in other parts of the continent. These close relatives, such as the kongoni (an East African hartebeest similar to the tsessebe), the yellow-spotted rock dassie and the yellow baboon, look similar, live in similar habitats and have similar habits, but to the scientist their differences, though often subtle, are sufficient for them to be classified as separate species.

Most species are now confined to areas of sanctuary, such as national parks and ever-diminishing areas of wilderness. Man has to manage these areas carefully to ensure that a healthy environment is maintained for all members of the animal and plant communities. Some large species, such as elephant and buffalo, must at times be culled to prevent their numbers rising above an area's ability to maintain a state of balance. A few species, such as the baboon, jackal and leopard, have been able to take advantage of man's presence, despite ruthless persecution, and are still widely distributed.

Species such as the black rhino have in recent years been drastically reduced in numbers and range because of intense poaching by man. The white rhino, on the other hand, has been brought back from extinction and is a rare success story in African conservation. The last few rhinos were protected in a nature reserve in Zululand and after careful management over the last 60 years have increased in number. The operation has been so successful that white rhinos can now be reintroduced to areas where they once used to roam. Sadly, the northern race of the white rhino was less fortunate and has also been methodically poached to the brink of extinction.

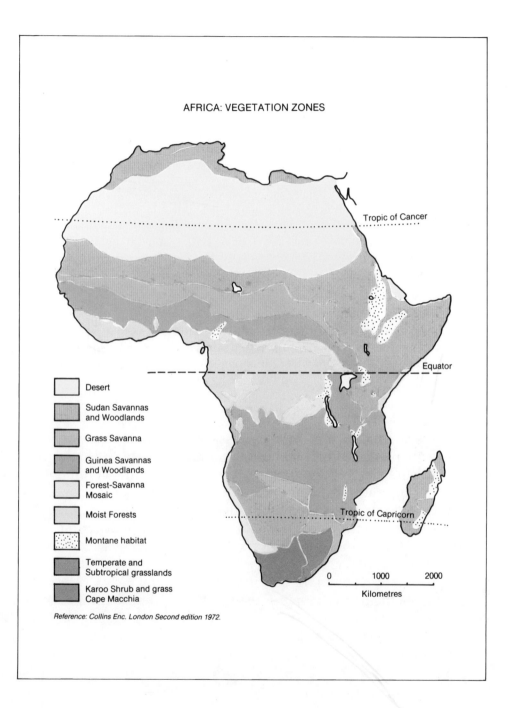

AFRICA: VEGETATION ZONES

Tropic of Cancer

Equator

Tropic of Capricorn

Desert

Sudan Savannas
and Woodlands

Grass Savanna

Guinea Savannas
and Woodlands

Forest-Savanna
Mosaic

Moist Forests

Montane habitat

Temperate and
Subtropical grasslands

Karoo Shrub and grass
Cape Macchia

0   1000   2000

Kilometres

Reference: Collins Enc. London Second edition 1972.

The maps offer a general guide to an animal's distribution. A species may not occur throughout large tracts of its range because of the activities of man, especially if the animal is considered a threat or as competition. To illustrate this, most species occurred down through to the Cape of Good Hope in South Africa when European settlers arrived four centuries ago, but because of hunting and persecution, very few large mammals now exist outside of a few national parks. The same pressure is being exerted on wildlife today in East Africa as the human population grows at alarming speed, displacing the once-teeming populations of plains wildlife.

It is interesting to compare the distribution of the various animals with the vegetation zones of Africa. A lot of information about the animals' habits and diet, etc., can be obtained from this simple exercise.

INFORMATION

The data on size, weight, lifespan, etc., are for an average specimen and, therefore are more representative than quoting Rowland Ward trophy sizes. This information should help one to appreciate differences in sizes and lifestyles of the various animals.

Note: Heights quoted are at the shoulder unless stated otherwise.

AFRICAN TRIBES

Though language, customs and dress can vary dramatically among the native peoples of Africa, a common ancestry can be traced in the folklore, which is remarkably similar throughout much of the continent. Thus, Umvundhla the Hare is the shady character of many a tale in many languages and dialects. It is thought that the tales of Brer Rabbit originated with the slaves transported to the New World from western Africa several centuries ago. This similarity between the tales and subjects is partially explained by the fact that the Bantu peoples of Africa originated from common roots in western central Africa. Over the past 2000 years the Bantu people spread further and further across central, eastern and southern Africa, conquering and assimilating the original inhabitants of these lands.

METRIC CONVERSIONS

For use in countries where the Metric system of measurement is used, the height and weight conversions for the different animals in the Facts sections are:

	Height		Weight		Weight at Birth	
	Male	Female	Male	Female	Male	Female
Lion	1m	90cm	200kg	130kg	——1.5kg——	
Leopard	75cm	70cm	70kg	60kg	——450g——	
Cheetah	75cm	75cm	60kg	55kg	——300g——	
Wild dog	65cm	65cm	30kg	25kg	——500g——	
Hyena	65cm	70cm	60kg	70kg	——1.5kg——	
Jackal	40cm	38cm	10kg	8kg	——200g——	
Elephant	3m	2.5m	5000kg	3500kg	——120kg——	
White Rhinoceros	1.8m	1.6m	3000kg	2000kg	——40kg——	
Black Rhinoceros	1.4m	1.2m	1500kg	1000kg	40kg	35kg
Hippopotamus	1.5m	1.2m	3000kg	2000kg	——30kg——	
Buffalo	1.6m	1.5m	700kg	600kg	——40kg——	
Baboon	1m	80cm	30kg	18kg	——250g——	
Giraffe	5.5m*	5m*	1200kg	900kg	——100kg——	
Waterbuck	1.3m	1.2m	250kg	200kg	——8kg——	
Zebra	1.2m	1.2m	320kg	280kg	——30kg——	
Tsessebe	1.2m	1.2m	160kg	145kg	——10kg——	
Wart hog	72cm	70cm	70kg	60kg	——800g——	
Hare	15cm	15cm	2.5kg	2kg	——80g——	
Dassie	20cm	20cm	4kg	3kg	250g	200g
Ostrich	2m	1.8m	140kg	120kg	——1.5kg——	
Tortoise	20cm	22cm	1.5kg	2kg	★	

(★ Length at hatching 4cm for both sexes)
(*Full height)

In the Beginning...

The Bushman believes that the Creator made the earth and then the plants upon it. Next, He thought up the many different animals which were to live in the world.

Striking a huge baobab tree, He caused the animals to walk into the light of day for the first time. As each one appeared through a great rent in the tree's roots, He named it and gave it a place to live. Even though He was assisted by Mantis, who was a super-being and the Creator's helper, the animals took a long time to come out of the tree and be named. Last of all came man.

By then, there was only one role left in the great scheme of things, so the Creator and Mantis assigned this place to the Bushman — that of Hunter-Gatherer. The Bushman fulfilled his designated role faithfully, living in close harmony with the animals, birds and the plants upon the earth.

Though the details of this story vary from tribe to tribe, they all record that the animals came before man.

According to Swazi folklore, animals all lived together in peace before the coming of man, and only when he finally appeared, did predation, or meat-eating, spread through the world. Man preyed upon beast; beasts then preyed upon their former friends — even the reptiles and birds copied the deadly example of man. With the coming of man into the world, so fear was born.

Why does the Lion Roar?

(A Batonka story)

After the coming of man into the world, Lion became the most feared of the predators. (As you will remember, the legend said that animals only started to eat meat after man arrived.) In these early days, Lion still had a gentle voice, not very loud at all, and so he was able to catch and eat the other animals without much trouble.

This, of course, greatly worried the other animals, since they never knew when Lion was on the hunt. They decided to hold a meeting to find a way of somehow making Lion less dangerous.

They talked for a long time, but none of them could think of anything. Hare, always the imaginative one, then had a bright idea.

"I know a way that would make Lion's voice like the terrible thunder of a summer's storm," he said, "and then we would always know when he was coming."

The other animals all agreed that this was a marvelous idea. But how was Hare going to manage such a thing? Hare just winked and set off on his difficult task.

Eventually Hare found Lion resting beneath a shady umbrella tree, and approaching him carefully, saying, "O Great One, I am truly most unhappy to bring you bad news, but your brother is very ill, and requests to see you at once." Lion was dreadfully upset to hear this news and told Hare to lead him to his brother as fast as possible.

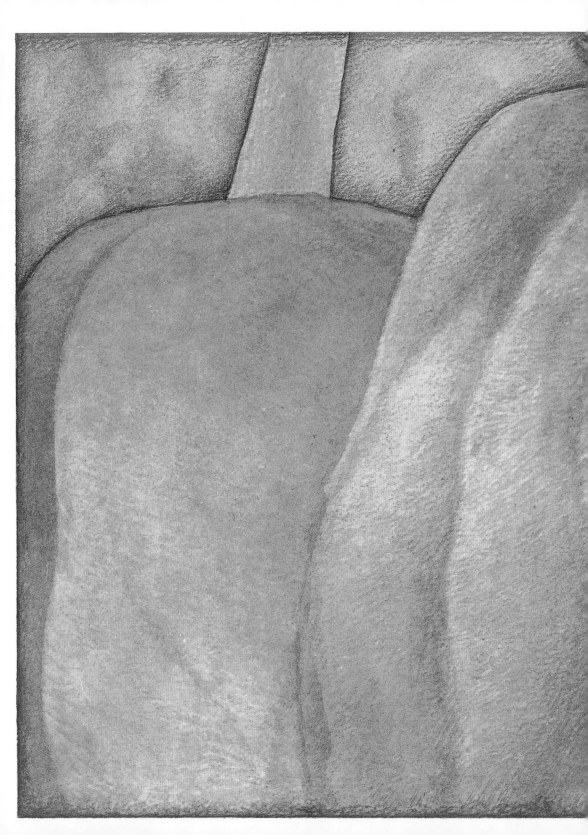

Hare took Lion for miles and miles around the Bushveld and after several hours Lion (who, after all, had been disturbed during his morning sleep) was so weary he could go no further. He lay down in a shady spot and slept.

Now, with the help of a honeyguide bird, the crafty Hare found a wild bees' nest in a tree not too far away. After following the required custom of leaving a good piece of the honeycomb as a "thank-you" for the little bird, Hare took some of the honey and dribbled it all over the paws and head of the sleeping lion. Hare then ran off to some thick bushes nearby and hid.

When the bees returned home and saw that someone had raided their hive, they were terribly angry. They soon found Lion sleeping nearby, with honey all over his paws. In a raging swarm, the bees attacked him, and Lion was stung so many times and was in such pain that his soft cries soon swelled to a thunderous roar that could be heard for miles around!

That is the story of how Lion's voice was changed forever. The animals were very grateful to Hare because, from then on, they could hear Lion's roar from a long way away, and be warned that the King of Beasts was on the hunt.

Why the Lion does not eat Fruit

(A Hambakushu story)

The Hambakush tribe of the Okavango region has this story that explains why Lion does not eat fruit (unless he is driven to it by extreme thirst).

M bwawa, the jackal, one day discovered the delicious fruit of the thaa tree. But as he sat there enjoying his meal, he heard Lion roaring in the distance. He thought to himself, "Lion sounds hungry. I hope he doesn't come this way and find all my lovely fruit." And he began to worry, since Lion, as everyone knows, has a huge appetite and, being the King of Beasts, is entitled to steal anyone's meal.

Lion did come near, but crafty Mbwawa had thought up a trick to stop Lion from eating his thaa fruit. As soon as Lion was near enough, Mbwawa began to eat the fruit as fast as he could, making sure Lion was watching this display of greed. Suddenly, Mbwawa collapsed in a heap on the ground, writhing and groaning, and then he lay still as if dead. Lion, of course, thought that the fruit must be poisonous, so he went on his way, and soon was out of sight.

Now Mbwawa, getting up, remembered where he had seen the skeleton of another jackal lying nearby. So he fetched it and placed it under the thaa tree on the spot where he had pretended to die. Well satisfied with his clever trick, he went home.

A few weeks later, Lion passed by and saw the thaa tree, laden with juicy-looking fruit. He walked over to the tree, but stopped when he saw the pitiful remains of a jackal. Its bones had been scattered by scavengers, and Lion then remembered seeing Mbwawa eating the fruit. He vowed to himself never to touch fruit again.

Since that day, Lion has never eaten the fruit of the thaa tree, or indeed of any other tree. This made the jackal, and all the other small animals of the bush, very happy. Now they could eat as much fruit as they wanted without having to share it with the lion's enormous appetite.

FACTS ABOUT LIONS
SPECIES:
LION *(Pantheia leo)*
Males often solitary.
Females live in family groups called prides with up to 12 adults.

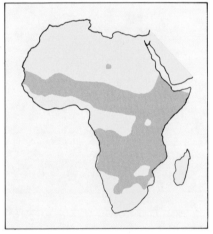

	Male	Female
Height	3⅓ ft	3 ft
Weight	440 lb	290 lb
Weight at Birth	3⅓ lb	3⅓ lb
Age at Weaning	8 months	8 months
Age at Maturity	4 years	3 years
Gestation Period	—	3½ months
Number of Young	—	2-5
Lifespan	20 years	20 years

Habitat All types of country except forest and mountain.
Habits Lions hunt singly, in pairs and in family parties. When harried they tend to become nocturnal, though normally they move and hunt during the cooler parts of the day, lying in shade during the heat between the hours of 10 a.m. and 4 p.m. Prides will combine to hunt, the males normally driving the prey

on to females waiting under cover where their remarkable powers of hiding enable them to blend with the background.

Unmolested they are seldom dangerous, particularly by day. However, they are always potentially aggressive because, being highly intelligent, they are also nervous, high strung and their moods can change with amazing speed.

Lions are the only kind of cat that live in groups (called prides). A pride is made up of females and their young, the cubs, and one fully-grown male lion, the pride leader.

The female lions stay with the pride all their lives, but not so the male lions; only the biggest and strongest one rules the pride. He is always suspicious of the young male lions who are growing up, in case they become stronger than he is, and he always drives them away from the pride before they are too big. This may seem cruel, but it is nature's way of making sure that the only lions to have cubs are the biggest, strongest ones, so that the cubs grow up big and strong too, and become good hunters in their turn.

When the young male lions are driven away, they either live alone or in small groups of "bachelor" lions. There they learn the ways of the bush, and how to kill for themselves. The best and strongest of them may be able to establish a pride of his own.

Lions normally drink every night, but when no rain falls for a long time they are surprisingly hardy. They go for days without water, but like every other animal in times of drought, they look out for juicy tsama melons and gemsbok cucumbers to keep them going.

Diet Lions are carnivorous, normally preying on buffalo, larger antelopes, zebra, ostriches, wild pigs, and occasionally giraffes and baby elephants. When desperately hungry, nothing is too small, and even man may provide a meal, though man-eating is comparatively rare. They will also raid stock when their normal food is scarce.

Breeding Breeding occurs throughout the year. The cubs, usually two to four to a litter, are born in thickets and other sheltered places as the mothers hide their young from the males, who are often aggressive to the cubs. When the cubs are very young the lioness hunts with the pride and returns to suckle her cubs. A group of lionesses will sometimes share looking after the larger cubs. Lions are polygamous; several lionesses may associate with one male and bear his cubs. Occasionally, two males may share one lioness but usually the more powerful drives the other away.

The Dreadful Crime of Kadima the Hare

(A Hambakushu story)

Once upon a time, say the Hambakush people, Kadima the hare had an agreement with Nthoo, the leopardess. In exchange for guarding the leopardess' three cubs while she was away hunting, Kadima was given a share of the kill for his supper.

This convenient arrangement worked very well until a hard drought came to the land. The wild animals which Nthoo hunted, all moved away to find water in other regions, and times became very hard for the leopardess, her cubs and Kadima. Day after day, Nthoo came home with nothing for them to eat, and soon they were starving.

Then, one day, Nthoo came home to find that Kadima was eating, and when questioned as to how he had come by the food when she, the finest hunter in the land, had failed to find anything, Kadima replied that a little duiker had wandered past the cave. He had managed to catch and kill it. But the truth was, that the meat that Kadima was eating was really one of the leopardess' cubs!

The next day Nthoo hunted again, and the wicked Kadima killed another of her cubs and ate it. When the leopardess returned empty-handed again that evening, she lay down wearily and asked Kadima to bring her cubs, so that they could be nursed. The crafty Kadima carried the one remaining cub to Nthoo three times, and so tricked her into believing all her cubs were alive and well.

The next morning, after Nthoo had departed, Kadima was so tempted by his hunger that he killed and ate the last leopard cub. To cover his crime he laid false trails to and from the cave, scratching up the undergrowth and breaking branches to make it look as though there had been a great fight.

Then he went down to the dried-up waterhole and painted himself bright red with ochre. When Nthoo returned home, he staggered towards her, weeping, and told her that her cubs had been killed by men who had carried them off to be eaten. He had tried to defend them, he said, but the hunters had beaten him off and he had almost bled to death from his wounds. And he pointed to the red stains on his fur.

Poor Nthoo! Her roar of grief and rage shook the heavens. In a terrible fury, she set off toward the nearest kraal, determined to take her revenge upon the people who had killed her children.

However, just as the leopardess was about to spring upon a group of young herd boys from the village, a loud voice cried out from the tree tops, "Nthoo!" It was the spy of the Bushveld, the Go-way bird. "Nthoo!" he screamed again. "Kadima was the wicked one who killed your children, not the good people of the village!"

Nthoo turned back in rage to seek out Kadima, but Kadima had heard the bird, and fled in terror.

Nthoo the leopardess never caught Kadima the hare, but it is said by the Hambakush people that she searches still.

That is why the leopardess is wary and now always hunts alone; and that is why the hare runs for its life without even looking back, if you should come upon it unawares.

Why the Leopard Hides his Food up a Tree

(A Ndebele story)

The Ndebele tell their children that long ago, there were three friends: the beautiful leopard, the jackal and the hyena. They went everywhere together. Whenever Leopard killed an animal, he would always leave part of it for his friends so that they could have a good feed too.

One day it happened that Leopard was ill, and so he could not hunt. "Jackal," he said, "Please catch some food for us, for I am not well."

But lazy Jackal said, "No. I am too weary. Ask Hyena."

So Leopard said, "Hyena, please hunt for us today, for I am not well enough to do so."

But Hyena, too, made an excuse: "No, I have a sore foot."

At this Leopard roared in anger. "I thought you were my friends, but you are a no-good, lazy pair. Never again will I leave you meat when I make my kill. From this day on, I will make sure of it. I shall take what is left and hang it in a tree, when I have eaten all I want. Then neither of you will be able to get at it."

Leopard was true to his word — for since that day he has never left any meat for his selfish friends. Up into a tree it goes, high out of reach of jackals and hyenas. They have become scavengers now instead, and they eat the scraps that other animals leave behind. It was a sad day for them when they lost Leopard's friendship.

FACTS ABOUT LEOPARDS

SPECIES:
LEOPARD *(Panthera pardus)*
Solitary.

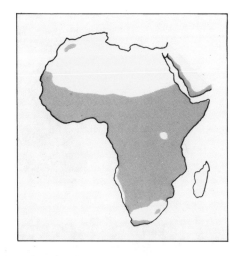

	Male	Female
Height	30 in	28 in
Weight	154 lb	132 lb
Weight at Birth	1 lb	1 lb
Age at Weaning	3 months	3 months
Age at Maturity	2 years	2 years
Gestation Period	—	3 months
Number of Young	—	2 or 3
Lifespan	15 years	15 years

Identification Leopards need not be confused with cheetahs because they are heavier, much more thick-set creatures with shorter legs and a look of great power. Their spots are different too, over most of the body occurring in clusters resembling a rosette whereas the cheetah's are quite separate.

Leopards' coats are a rich, dark sandy-yellow on top graduating to pure white at the throat, inside of the legs and underside of the body. The spots are black.

In high mountain areas leopards occasionally are black all over.

Habitat Leopards live in a wide variety of terrain, from high mountains and rocky country to forest and grasslands and even semi-desert.

Habits Being nocturnal, very wary and elusive, leopards are not often seen. They tend to be solitary and hunt alone although male and female move around together during the mating season.

Leopards often hide up trees during the day, or among rocks, in thick bush, in caves and even in wart hog holes!

When hunting they often lie silently on a tree branch above a game trail and then drop, claws extended, on to the back of the unsuspecting victim. These claws can be fully retracted into the paws, as with all true cats.

Diet Leopards' main prey are impala, but they have a remarkably varied diet which includes insects, fishes, frogs, birds, hyenas, dogs and baboons, which they seem to regard as a particular delicacy.

Breeding There is no particular breeding season. Up to six cubs may be born but the norm is two or three.

How Cheetah got his Speed

(A Bushman story)

Once upon a time the Creator decided to find out which of His animals could run the fastest — and so He entered the cheetah in a race with the tsessebe, which is the swiftest of all the antelopes. The cheetah had soft paws then, and he realized that they were not suited for real speed. So he borrowed a set of paws from an obliging wild dog.

The race started from a high baobab tree. The Creator Himself was in charge, and the two contestants were told to run right across the plains to a hill on the far side. The animals lined up, and then — go! They leapt away.

The tsessebe soon took the lead, and by half-way, he was so far ahead he seemed sure to win. But suddenly — disaster! Tsessebe stumbled on a stone and crashed to the ground; he had broken his leg.

The good-natured cheetah, instead of running past and winning the race, stopped to help his opponent.

The Creator, seeing this, was so pleased by the cheetah's unselfish act that He bestowed upon the cheetah a gift; He made him the fastest animal in the land; and what's more, allowed him to keep the paws of the wild dog.

Why the Cheeks of the Cheetah are Stained with Tears

(A Zulu story)

Long ago, a wicked and lazy hunter was sitting under a tree, gazing idly at a large clearing below where a herd of fat springbok were peacefully grazing. The hunter was thinking that it was far too hot to bother himself with a long and tiring stalk through the bushes, when suddenly he noticed a movement off to the right. It was a female cheetah which had also chosen this herd to hunt — and she was doing it very well.

Keeping downwind of the herd, she was moving closer to them very slowly, inch by inch, and keeping well under cover. The hunter watched, fascinated, as she crept closer and closer to a springbok which had unwisely wandered away from the main herd.

Suddenly, she gathered her long legs under her, and sprang forward like an arrow. With dazzling speed she raced down upon the springbok and caught it just as it started to leap away.

Panting from her effort, the cheetah dragged her prize away to some shade on the edge of the clearing. The hunter watched, marveling at the speed

and skill he had just witnessed. But as he watched, he saw to his surprise that three beautiful cheetah cubs had also been watching and waiting in the shade.

Now the hunter was filled with envy for the cubs, and wished that he, too, could have such a good hunter to provide for him. This gave him a wicked idea; he knew that cheetahs never attack men, and so he decided that it would be easy to take one of the cubs and train it to hunt for him. Chuckling to himself, he settled down to wait. (After all, he was cowardly too, and did not wish to find out whether a mother cheetah would defend her cubs.)

When the sun was setting, the mother cheetah left her cubs concealed in a bush, and set off to the waterhole to drink. Quickly, the hunter grabbed his spear and trotted down to the bushes where the cubs were hidden. There he found the three cubs, still too young to run away. He could not decide which one to take, and so he stole them all, thinking to himself that three cheetahs would undoubtedly be better than one.

When their mother came back half an hour later and found her babies gone, she was broken-hearted. The poor mother cheetah cried and cried, until her tears made dark stains down her cheeks. She wept all night, and all the next day. She cried so loudly that she was heard by an old man, who came to see what all the noise was about.

Now, it so happened that this old man was very wise in the ways of the world, and he had a great knowledge of, and respect for, animals. When he found out what had happened, he became very angry, for not only had the lazy hunter become a thief, but he had broken the traditions of the tribe. All knew that a hunter must use only his own strength and skill. Any other way of hunting was surely a dishonor.

The old man returned to the village and told the other elders what had happened. The villagers became angry, too, and the people found the lazy hunter and drove him away from the village for ever.

The old man took the three cheetah cubs and returned them to their grateful mother; but the long weeping of the mother cheetah had stained her face permanently, and so, to this day, say the Zulu, the cheetah wears the tearstains on its face as a reminder to the hunters that it is not honorable to hunt in any other way than that which is traditional.

FACTS ABOUT CHEETAHS
SPECIES:
CHEETAH *(Acinonyx jubatus)*
Solitary.
ENDANGERED SPECIES

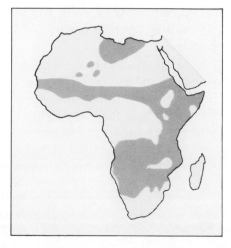

	Male	Female
Height	30 in	30 in
Weight	132 lb	121 lb
Weight at Birth	10 oz	10 oz
Age at Weaning	3 months	3 months
Age at Maturity	2 years	2 years
Gestation Period	—	3 months
Number of Young	—	2-4
Lifespan	10 years	10 years

Identification The cheetah has a lighter body and much longer legs than the leopard, though its overall length is similar. Its spots are different, occurring as individual solid black spots rather than the clusters that characterize the leopard's coat. The cheetah is built for high speed over short distances and even *looks* like a sprinter.

The coat is a similar color to that of the leopard; from dark sandy-yellow on top to pure white under the body and inside the legs. The single black spots occur all over the head, body and legs, blending into bands around the tip of the tail.

Habitat Cheetahs usually live in open country and are very rarely, if ever, found in thick forest.

Habits Widely believed to be the fastest animal on earth, the cheetah has a top speed of around 62 miles per hour (100 km per hour). Its dog-like claws, which do not fully retract like those of a true cat, assist it to reach these speeds by improving grip — like spiked running shoes. These high speeds can only be maintained for relatively short distances — no more than 360 feet. It uses its speed to catch quarry after a short sprint, having first crept up silently. But once winded, the cheetah must give up the chase and look for some other animal.

Having grabbed their prey by the throat, knocked it down and killed it, cheetahs bolt down large quantities of meat very quickly, probably to avoid having it stolen by other predators. Cheetahs will not defend their food and this timid characteristic means they often lose their kills to lions, hyenas and sometimes even vultures. This competition for food often results in a high mortality of cubs and young cheetahs.

They are generally solitary and families separate quickly once the cubs have matured.

Diet Medium-sized buck, such as impala, are the cheetah's usual food, though wart hog, guinea-fowl, hares and even ostriches are also taken.

Breeding Two or three cubs are usually born. They are especially beautiful, with long, silver-gray fur. The mother calls to them in a very un-catlike way — with a high-pitched whistle like a bird.

The Revenge of Wild Dog

(A Ndebele story)

Long ago, Wild Dog was very happy, as he possessed a lovely den, a good wife and many children.

Wild Dog was much respected by the animals of the bush, so that when his wife fell ill one day, his cousin Jackal was most concerned. Jackal took Wild Dog to see Hare, for Hare knew the remedies for most ailments.

Hare threw the bones and said that Wild Dog's wife was seriously ill and would get worse. He had a medicine that would make her better, but they could not touch it. They were told to return to the sick wife and tend to her comfort. Hare would see to it that the muti (medicine) would get to them.

Hare then spent all morning preparing the medicine and when he had finished, he called Duiker and told him to carry the medicine in a calabash to the den of Wild Dog. Hare warned Duiker that on no account was he to look back, as that would make the muti useless.

Duiker set off, but on his way he heard trees being broken behind him and, without thinking, he turned around to look. The medicine spilled onto the ground.

Hare was very disappointed to hear Duiker's story, but he prepared some more medicine, and this time he sent Impala on the errand. Impala was given the same warning, but halfway there he was startled by the scent of a lion, looked behind him, and — crash! The calabash fell to the ground and was smashed.

Now, for the third time Hare made up the muti, and this time Zebra volunteered for the task as he felt he was strong and steady enough to handle it.

So Zebra set off, determined to succeed where the smaller animals had failed. He trotted steadily along, and twice along the way heard frightening noises behind him. But he remembered the warning, and ignored them bravely.

Zebra had nearly reached the den of Wild Dog, when suddenly between his front hooves a deadly black mamba reared up, hissing. Zebra jumped and kicked out, terrified of being bitten. Before he could remember Hare's warning, he panicked, turned, and ran for home. As he did so, the calabash fell to the ground and broke into many pieces. Just as this happened, Zebra heard cries and wails of grief coming from Wild Dog's den. The sick wife had waited too long for the medicine and had finally died.

Wild Dog was so distraught with sorrow that he called his family and friends together in a large pack, and together they chased Zebra for many miles. When they caught him they tore him to pieces.

Ever since that time, wild dogs have hunted together in packs. The zebra and impala have always been their special prey, for they have never forgotten the story of the precious medicine that would have saved Wild Dog's beloved wife.

FACTS ABOUT WILD DOGS
SPECIES:
WILD DOG *(Lycaon pictus)*

Gregarious, found in large packs of up to 30.

ENDANGERED SPECIES

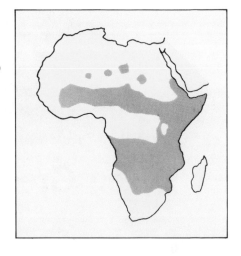

	Male	Female
Height	26 in	26 in
Weight	66 lb	55 lb
Weight at Birth	18 oz	18 oz
Age at Weaning	3 months	3 months
Age at Maturity	12 years	8 years
Gestation Period	—	2 months
Number of Young	—	2-8
Lifespan	10 years	10 years

Identification The large, erect, forward-facing, rounded ears are the most obvious feature of the "Wild," "Hunting" or "Cape Hunting" dog. The dogs are covered in hair which varies greatly in color; no two dogs have the same markings. However, all have a distinctive dark brown or black muzzle and lower face, and a white brush at the tip of the tail.

Habitat The wild dog roams and hunts in open grasslands and light woodlands.

Habits They live in packs of up to 30 and have a well-organized social structure. For example, one or two females will act as "baby-sitters" to several litters of pups while the rest of the pack go hunting.

Old, sick and pregnant members of the pack are also cared for, which is quite unusual as far as the old and sick are concerned in the animal world.

Their hunting technique is also unusually sophisticated. They select a particular animal in the quarry herd, probably one that is sick or disabled. Two or three dogs will then chase it hard, the others loping easily on the flanks or behind. Whenever the "chaser" dogs tire, their place is taken by fresher dogs and this continues until the prey can no longer outrun its hunters.

Diet Wild dogs prey on a wide variety of game, from large animals like zebra down to small antelopes. They sometimes kill livestock and because of this and the way they hunt, man tends to regard them as killers. In reality they perform the important task of culling sick animals before infection can spread.

Breeding A number of pregnant bitches will often give birth together in a special lair, either a deserted anteater hole or other similar shelter.

The Greedy Hyena

(A Shona story)

One fine day, Hyena went out hunting. It was the dry season, so animals were scarce and Hyena was very hungry because he hadn't eaten for several days.

After much searching, Hyena suddenly saw an impala doe and her new fawn. Crouching low, behind a tuft of long grass, Hyena started to think about the fine meal that the young impala would make. He began to drool, and his stomach rumbled quite pleasantly.

"But," he thought, "that mother impala is going to be a bit of a problem." She had no horns, of course, being a female impala, but still she could surely put up quite a fight with her sharp hooves. Hyena decided that if he could kill the mother first, the tender young fawn would then be an easy catch.

So Hyena jumped out from his hiding place and charged straight at the mother impala. She sped off at a fair pace, leading her attacker away from her baby, which ran away in another direction.

After several miles, with the mother impala keeping just out of reach, Hyena realized that she was simply leading him a chase which he could never hope to win. He would never catch the swift impala, and as she disappeared over yet another ridge, he gave up the chase.

"Aha," he thought to himself, "the little fawn is all alone now, and if I hurry back, I'll have my supper before the sun goes down."

Hyena loped back to the starting point, confident that he could easily take the baby impala. But on reaching the place where the chase had

started, Hyena was dismayed to find that the fawn was nowhere to be seen — it had gone back to the safety of the herd, under the watchful eye of its father, the magnificent herd ram. The baby was now waiting for its mother to return from her little jaunt.

Hyena searched about for a long while, but he finally realized that he had foolishly tried to do something that was too difficult for him. If he hadn't been so greedy, trying to catch both the mother and her fawn, he would not have gone to bed hungry that night.

FACTS ABOUT HYENAS

SPECIES:

SPOTTED HYENA (*Crocuta crocuta*)

Gregarious, living in groups of up to 12, called clans.

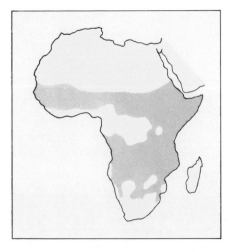

	Male	Female
Height	26 in	28 in
Weight	132 lb	154 lb
Weight at Birth	3⅓ lb	3⅓ lb
Age at Weaning	12 months	12 months
Age at Maturity	2 years	2 years
Gestation Period	—	3 months
Number of Young	—	2-4
Lifespan	20 years	20 years

Identification The most prominent features of the spotted hyena are a large head in proportion to its body, large rounded ears, a sloping back and a short, bushy tail held erect. Its short, coarse coat is a reddish to grayish color with irregular dark spots.

Habitat Hyenas are found in almost every type of country from desert fringes to the snowline.

Habits Because of their gruesome habits and unnerving cries they figure in many African tribes' superstitious beliefs. In fact they are very clever animals with excellent sight, smell and hearing. They watch for vultures in the sky circling over a kill and use them as guides. A clan of hyenas may even be brave enough to chase a pride of lions off their kill.

They either roam singly or in pairs to scavenge, or the clan will organize into efficient packs and hunt prey as large as wildebeest and greater kudu.

Diet They are predominantly scavengers, cleaning up the remains of kills left by other animals and thereby performing a very important ecological function. They have immensely powerful jaws and very strong teeth, and so can easily crunch up massive thigh bones and skulls and devour hides. However, they also hunt their own food.

Breeding At mating, large parties of hyenas assemble and make the most terrible racket, often in moonlight.

Up to four pups are born, usually in old aardvark holes or sheltered places. The cubs, particularly the females, remain within the family clan. They are dependent on their mothers for up to 24 months, weaning at 6 months.

The Tree-climbing Jackal

(A story from Swaziland)

Jackal was well-known for playing tricks on his fellow creatures, so they mistrusted him; but in spite of this, he fooled them time and again. The animals also disliked Jackal because he was a most annoying boaster.

Now one day, while out hunting for food, Jackal met Wildcat, who was lounging elegantly on the branch of a tree. Jackal was jealous, as this was something he could not do.

"Why do you climb trees, Wildcat?" he asked.

Wildcat replied that it gave her an excellent view, so that she could see friend or foe coming from a long way off. Also, climbing trees was a handy way of escaping from the dogs which were forever chasing her.

"Oh, what a coward you are, Wildcat!" sneered the jackal. "Only cowards, snakes and silly birds hide in trees."

Wildcat's feelings were hurt, but she kept her temper, knowing that Jackal was a nasty trickster, and thinking it would be better to keep on the right side of him.

"Do not forget," she replied patiently, "I cannot run as fast as you, and dogs are my natural enemy."

"I can run faster than any creature in the land," boasted Jackal. "Let those scruffy old dogs come — I'm not afraid of them — anyway, I could outrun them any day."

"That may be so," replied Wildcat gently, "but the art of climbing trees has its use in times of trouble, you know. Would you like me to teach you?"

Jackal considered this generous offer. "Hmm ... Well, knowledge can never hurt one," he replied airily, "and I've nothing better to do at the moment." Secretly, he was rather anxious to learn.

Wildcat came down from her branch, and Jackal was given his first lesson. But alas, he was not a very good pupil because his claws were too blunt to grip the bark. He kept slipping, and falling on his back in the dirt.

Polite as she was, Wildcat could not help laughing at the sight of Jackal, the oh-so-clever one, scrabbling furiously up the trunk of the tree and falling in a heap every time.

Jackal was getting angrier and angrier, and suddenly he flew into a rage. He turned and snapped at poor Wildcat, grabbing her leg and snarling that he would kill her for making him look ridiculous.

That would most certainly have been the end of Wildcat, but, fortunately for her, a pack of dogs suddenly appeared, barking furiously. Jackal took one look and instantly was no longer the brave animal of his boasting.

He let go of Wildcat's leg and, as she scrambled up her tree to safety, Jackal put his tail between his legs and ran. He dived down a nearby anteater hole just as the dogs were about to catch him. The dogs tried to dig him out, but they could not reach him, so after a while they gave up and went away.

Now Jackal crept out of the hole and, to his shame, saw Wildcat grinning down at him from her perch. She burst out laughing as he slunk away to mend his wounded pride.

From that day on, whenever Wildcat happened to see Jackal, she took refuge in the nearest tree, for Jackal never forgot how she had seen his cowardice, and his desire for revenge was truly something to fear.

How Jackal got his Markings

(A Hottentot story)

The Hottentot used to tell how eventually even the Creator became angry at the slyness of Jackal, and at the way he would always torment the other animals with his tricks. So the Creator decided to punish him. He appeared before Jackal one day, disguised as a young boy.

The "boy" persuaded Jackal to give him a ride on his back. He said that he was lost, and was too tired to walk any further. If Jackal would help him to find his village, he said, he would reward him with a tender young goat when they got there.

So Jackal allowed the "boy" to climb upon his back, and set off, already planning to himself how he could trick the "boy" into giving him not only one goat, but the whole herd.

Suddenly, he felt the "boy's" legs grip his back with a terrible force. "I am the Creator!" cried the "boy," and he produced a ball of fire. "And this is my punishment to you for all your wicked ways!" So saying, He struck Jackal on his flanks with the fire, which set the animal's coat ablaze.

Jackal begged for mercy, but the Creator disappeared, leaving the ball of fire on Jackal's back. Jackal rolled desperately, and finally managed to put out the flames. Then he went on his way, much shaken and humbled.

And that is why, to this day, the jackal has black marks along his body, and silver "ashes" on his back — so that all the animals can see that he was punished by the Creator for his wicked ways.

The Day Jackal Fooled the King of Beasts

(A Zulu story)

This is a Zulu folk tale, and shows exactly the sort of thing that clever old Jackal would get up to.

One day long ago, Jackal was trotting through a narrow and rocky pass when he came face to face with Lion, who was coming in the opposite direction. Realizing that he was too near to escape, Jackal was afraid, for he had played many tricks on Lion in the past, and now Lion might take this opportunity to get his revenge.

In a flash, he thought of a plan. He cowered down on the cliff path, looked above him, and cried, "Help!"

Lion stopped short in surprise. He had indeed been just about to leap upon Jackal and give him the beating of his life.

"Help!" cried Jackal again, "The rocks are about to fall on us! We shall both be crushed! Do something, O mighty Lion!"

Lion looked up too, most alarmed, but before he had time to think, Jackal was begging him to use his great strength to hold up an overhanging rock.

"Hold on!" cried Jackal, "I'll run and fetch that log over there to prop under the rock — then we'll both be saved!"

Lion put his great shoulder to the rock and heaved. While sneering Jackal made his escape, Lion was left all alone to struggle under the weight of the unmoving rock.

How long he remained there before he realized that it had all been yet another trick, we will never know. But one thing is perfectly clear: Jackal had to be twice as wary of Lion from that day forward.

FACTS ABOUT JACKALS
SPECIES:
BLACK-BACKED JACKAL
(Canis mesomelas)
Live singly or, more commonly, in pairs.

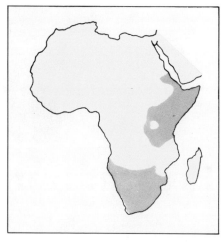

	Male	Female
Height	16 in	15 in
Weight	22 lb	18 lb
Weight at Birth	7 oz	7 oz
Age at Weaning	2 months	2 months
Age at Maturity	12 months	8 months
Gestation Period	—	2 months
Number of Young	—	2-6
Lifespan	10 years	10 years

Identification Not unlike a European fox, though larger and taller, the black-backed jackal is easily distinguished from other jackals by the broad black-and-white patch over its back, which is clearly defined from the yellowish covering on the flanks and legs. It has a bushy tail with a black brush and large, pointed, erect ears.

Habitat Open grassland and lightly-treed country.

Habits Jackals are common all over Africa. They are mostly nocturnal and their distinctive, rather friendly howling call can often be heard at dusk or just after. They are very wily animals and run quickly and lightly. They live with a mate or alone, and hunt from a lair in a sheltered hole, usually near water.

They are "true" dogs, with five toes on the front feet and four on the back. Some zoologists believe many domestic dogs are descended from them.

Diet Jackals scavenge and hunt. They eat such things as small rats, ground-nesting birds and their eggs and chicks; reptiles, fat insects and fruit. They will also kill newly born antelopes left unattended by the mother; and attack young livestock, so farmers regard them as pests to be shot, though they have their good side, keeping down pests like rats. They are often seen waiting for lions to finish eating so they can clean up the remains. The more venturesome will try and dart in to steal tidbits from under the lion's nose! Their clever ways have been the subject of many tales throughout Africa.

Breeding Usually no more than six pups are born. The parents hide them in holes in the ground and crevices in rocks. Both parents forage at the weaning stage and provide them with regurgitated, semi-digested food.

Elephant Learns some Manners

(A Shona story)

One day Elephant came across Squirrel on the path to the river. The proud and lordly Elephant swept Squirrel off the path with his trunk, rumbling, "Out of my way, you of no importance and tiny size."

Squirrel was most offended, as he had every right to be. Stamping his little feet in a rage, he decided that he was going to try and teach Elephant some manners.

"Ho!" shouted Squirrel indignantly, "you may be very tall, and you may be very proud, and I bet you think you're the greatest animal on earth, but you're much mistaken!"

Elephant looked round in surprise. "I am not mistaken, Squirrel," he rumbled, "I am the greatest, and everyone knows it."

"Let me tell you something, Elephant," said Squirrel, chittering angrily and flicking his tail, "I may be small, but I can eat ten times as much as you! I challenge you to an eating contest — and I bet you that I, Squirrel, can eat more palm nuts, and for a longer time, than you, high and mighty Elephant!"

Elephant roared with laughter. He was so amused, in fact, that he accepted the tiny creature's challenge. Besides, he was rather fond of palm nuts.

So both animals collected a huge pile of palm nuts and agreed to start the contest the very next morning, at first light. Elephant could hardly wait. He even skipped his evening meal of acacia pods so as to be truly empty for the morning. He intended to put Squirrel firmly in his place, once and for all.

The next day dawned fine and sunny, as it often does in Africa, and the two contestants started to eat.

Elephant munched steadily through his pile, with a fine appetite. Squirrel, nibbling away furiously, was soon full to bursting. Quietly, he slipped away, sending a cousin who was hiding nearby to take his place. Elephant was so absorbed in his greedy task that he didn't even notice. Brothers, sisters, cousins, uncles, aunts — one hungry squirrel after another took a turn at the pile of palm nuts.

Eventually, at midday, Elephant looked up. "Well, Squirrel, have you had enough yet?" he asked, surprised to see his small adversary still busily eating. Not only was he still eating, but his pile of palm nuts was disappearing almost as fast as Elephant's own.

"Not yet!" mumbled Squirrel, his mouth full, "and you?"

"Never!" replied Elephant scornfully. And he started to eat a little faster.

By the time the sun was setting, Elephant was so full he could hardly stand. He looked over to where Squirrel (the original squirrel, who had come back after a day of sleeping in a nearby tree), was still eating more palm nuts. Elephant groaned.

"Truly you are amazing, Squirrel," he said. "I cannot go on, and I'm forced to admit that you have won the contest." And he lifted his trunk in salute.

Squirrel, hopping with delight, thanked Elephant and told him not to be so proud in future. And from that day to this, Elephant has always shown great respect for Squirrel.

The Elephant and the Rain

(An ancient Bushman story)

There were once two great powers in the natural world: Elephant, and the Spirit of Rain. Now Elephant, who as you know was proud and boastful, was always arguing with Rain, trying to make him agree that of the two of them, he, Elephant, was the greater.

One day they were arguing as usual, when the Rain Spirit said, in his wet, gurgling voice, "How can you, Elephant, be a greater power than I, when it is I who nourishes you?"

Elephant was far too proud to admit that Rain was right. Indeed, he didn't even think before replying, "You do not feed me! I find my food for myself. I am my own master in all things."

Rain, angered in earnest this time, decided to act, instead of arguing any further. He turned dark gray, thundered, and said, "If I go away, will you not die?" And then he vanished.

Once Rain had departed, Elephant laughed loudly and said to himself, "Ha! Now I may rule alone. Rain has admitted defeat by running away!"

For many months, Elephant lorded it over the plains and forests, and life continued normally. In fact, it was quite peaceful without the constant loud quarrels of Elephant and Rain.

Then the time of year for the rains arrived. Many of the animals were full with their unborn young ones. Every animal was looking forward to the flush of green grass, and clean, flowing rivers once again.

But, of course, Rain had gone away. The skies remained hot and bright blue. Not even a cloud was seen for weeks. The animals became worried because their newborn young were starving.

In great distress, they went to find Elephant, for was he not their Lord? Elephant looked a bit uncomfortable, but he replied to their demands by saying, "I will call Vulture, the most potent of all the rainmakers."

Elephant then called Vulture and commanded him to cast lots and make rain. But Vulture was Rain's servant, and knew about the quarrel that the two mighty ones had had. He excused himself, explaining to Elephant that he was too afraid of the great Elephant to try, in case he failed.

Elephant then summoned Crow, the wisest of all birds, and commanded her to cast lots to make rain. This she did, and some rain fell. Enough rain fell to fill a few pans, but soon they all dried up, except one, the deepest.

Elephant claimed this last waterhole for himself, and ordered Tortoise to guard it for him while he was away feeding during the day (food was becoming rather difficult to find). Tortoise settled down to guard the pan.

Soon, a herd of giraffe came down to drink and asked Tortoise for water, for they had searched all day and found none. But Tortoise had to refuse, saying the pan was the property of Lord Elephant. Zebras, gemsbok, wildebeest, tsessebe, springboks and many other animals were all in turn refused a drink. They moved off in distance, whispering among themselves and wondering what was to become of them.

In the evening, Lion came down to drink and, as before, Tortoise told him he could not as the pan belonged to Elephant. But Lion was not impressed. He simply cuffed Tortoise out of the way and drank his fill. Poor

Tortoise was helpless, as the other animals, made desperate by thirst, followed Lion's example. They crowded around the pan and drank deeply.

When Elephant returned, the animals had drunk the pan dry, leaving only a mass of churned-up mud. He trumpeted in rage, and turned upon the unfortunate Tortoise. Poor Tortoise tried to explain that he had been too little and weak to stop the thirsty animals, but Elephant was in such a rage that he picked up Tortoise and swallowed him whole.

Now Tortoise did not want to die, especially since he did not deserve such punishment. As soon as he reached Elephant's stomach, he began to tear at the soft insides, determined to get out.

Elephant screamed with pain, and realized at the same time that his pride and arrogance had led him to a nasty end. By the time Tortoise managed to get out, Elephant was dead. Tortoise scuttled off as fast as he could, and ever since, he has refused to answer to anyone. He is his own master, and he goes wherever he likes.

The Rain Spirit, seeing that the tragic lesson had been learned by all the animals, took pity on the thirsty earth and poured down in a deluge, so that all the rivers and pans filled up again.

FACTS ABOUT ELEPHANTS
SPECIES:
AFRICAN ELEPHANT (*Loxodonta africana*)

Males often solitary. Females live in family groups and temporary herds of up to 200.

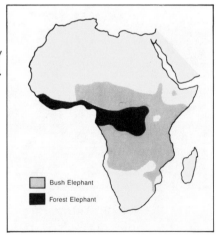

	Male	Female
Height	10 ft	9 ft
Weight	11000 lb	7700 lb
Weight at Birth	264 lb	264 lb
Age at Weaning	2 years	2 years
Age at Maturity	16 years	14 years
Gestation Period	—	22 months
Number of Young	—	1
Lifespan	55 years	70 years

Bush Elephant
Forest Elephant

Identification Elephants are the largest land animals in the world and it is interesting to note the difference between African and Asian elephants: the latter is smaller in stature, has much smaller ears and only the males have tusks. Also, Asian elephants can be tamed and used to work and entertain. These things have rarely been done successfully with African elephants.

Habitat Elephants can be found in grassy, open woodland, deep forest and quite high on the slopes of mountains as long as the ground is not too steep and broken.

Habits Highly organized socially, they live in family groups of 10-20, each ruled by a mature female.

When young bulls are old enough to look after themselves, they form separate temporary "bachelor" herds and fight among themselves to establish the strongest which will eventually return to the family herds to find a mate. This ensures only the strongest animals become fathers. The old bulls often live singly or in pairs and never rejoin the herd.

Family herds will join together in large groups at times of drought, and migrate together. Herds often travel great distances at night and spend a great deal of their time feeding. Elephants love water and are good swimmers. An adult will consume 22 gallons (100 litres) at one time! After their daily drink, they will spend an hour or two splashing, spraying water with their trunks, playing and wallowing in the mud, frequently dusting themselves with fine sand, in much the same way as we use talcum powder!

Elephants will dig deep holes in dry riverbeds, waiting patiently for the water to seep through to give a trunkful to drink. This is useful to other animals, which use the holes after the elephants.

The elephant's trunk is a marvelous tool used for feeding, drinking, stripping bark, smelling the air, picking fruit, and many other things. It is also a formidable weapon if need be, though a mature elephant has no natural enemies. A charging elephant can reach speeds of 25 miles per hour (40 km per hour) over short distances.

Diet Elephants graze and browse, going through up to 660 lbs (300 kg) of food a day, mostly grass. They also eat a variety of leaves, flowers, fruit, roots and tree bark, and in a normal lifespan will grow six sets of teeth! Their habit of pushing over trees to reach a few mouthfuls of young green leaves at the top (or roots at the bottom) can make them wasteful feeders.

Breeding When birth is imminent the cow leaves the herd, often with two or three attendant cows who help look after the baby until it is strong enough to walk back to the herd with its mother after a few days.

Why Rhino scatters his Dung

(A Batonka story)

In days long ago, when animals could talk, Elephant used to tease Rhino about his nearsightedness and bad temper (which was not very fair, since Elephant himself has not got the world's best eyesight, nor is he the most sweet-tempered of Africa's characters). Anyway, Elephant was teasing Rhino and sure enough, after a while Rhino could not help himself — he lost his temper. He challenged Elephant to a contest. (Rhino was quite sure he could win, and so prove that he was better than Elephant in at least one way.) The contest was to see who could produce the largest dung-heap.

Now both animals are large, they both eat vast quantities of vegetation each day, and of course they both make a lot of dung. But Rhino made by far the largest heap, as old Elephant soon found out.

Rhino's pride at beating Elephant was short-lived, however. Elephant was a poor loser, and he flew into a jealous rage that was worse than anything even Rhino had been known to have. In his fury, he attacked Rhino and beat him savagely with his trunk, goring him with his tusks until Rhino begged for mercy.

"O Elephant," pleaded Rhino, "Stop! I was mistaken. You are the greatest of creatures. You win. Only stop!" Poor Rhino lay on his back in the dust, wailing in fear.

Gradually, Elephant's great fury began to wear off, and he made Rhino beg and plead and promise never again to challenge the might of the Lord of the Beasts, namely himself, Elephant. At last he was satisfied and let poor Rhino escape.

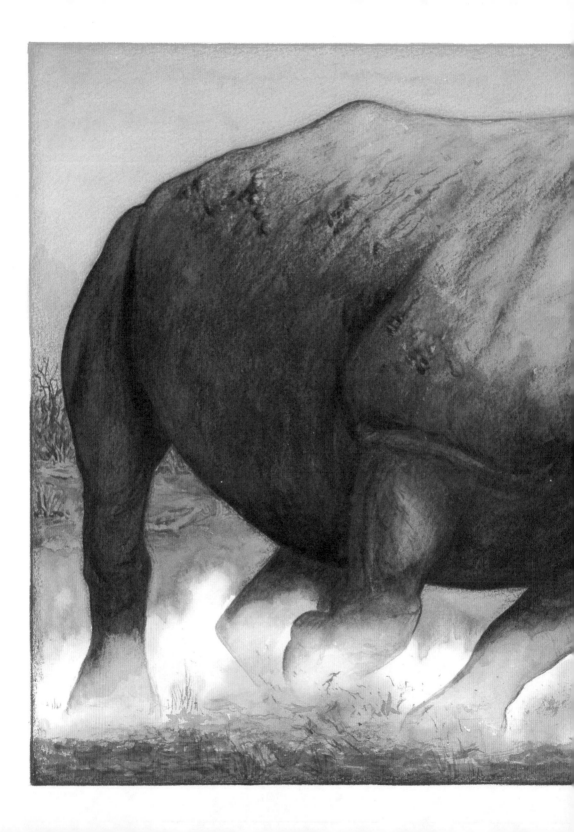

Rhino never forgot that dreadful beating, and he is afraid he may receive another one, so he makes sure that his dung-heap always looks smaller than that of Elephant. And this is why he kicks at it, scattering it until it is quite flat.

The Lost Quill

(A Ndebele story)

Once, in ancient times, Elephant and Rhino had a little argument which led to a big fight (both were short-tempered animals, as you now well know). Rhino fought bravely and wounded Elephant several times with his sharp horn; but his bad temper and rage made him fight rather blindly.

Elephant, however, kept his temper under control and, because he was much bigger and stronger, and could use his long tusks, he was soon winning. Eventually, Rhino had to give in. Bruised and torn, with a great many gashes in his thick hide, he limped away.

Rhino was in great pain, and bleeding badly. He sought out Porcupine, whom he thought might be able to help him. He begged her to give him one of her longest and strongest quills so that he could use it as a needle and sew up the great tears in his skin.

Porcupine, who was not too happy about being awakened from her daytime sleep, was anxious to get back to bed, and so to get rid of Rhino she agreed to lend him her best quill on one condition: that Rhino would return it when he had finished with it. She also felt rather sorry for Rhino.

"My quills," she squeaked, "are all I have to protect me against my enemy, Lion. So I am depending on you, Rhino, to bring that quill back."

Rhino solemnly agreed to this and gave her his word that he would return the quill the very next day.

Rhino sewed up his torn skin, using fiber from a baobab tree. (To this day, you can still see the rough, scarred ridges on his hide.) Satisfied with his handiwork, he lay down in some soft grass for a much-needed, healing sleep. He placed Porcupine's quill carefully beside him for safekeeping.

One evening a few days later, Rhino happened to meet Porcupine. He suddenly remembered his promise, but try as he might, he just couldn't remember where he had left the quill, or what had become of it. All he remembered was sewing himself up with the quill held in his mouth. "Goodness me!" he thought, "Could I have swallowed it by mistake?"

After a great deal of thought, Rhino came to the conclusion that if he had swallowed the quill, then sooner or later it would meet the same fate as all the other things that he swallowed each day. He explained all this to Porcupine, and apologized, promising soon to return the quill.

And that is why Rhino began to kick his dung about: he has been searching ever since in the hope of finding that lost porcupine quill among his droppings.

FACTS ABOUT RHINOCEROS
SPECIES:
WHITE RHINOCEROS *(Ceratotherium simum,* syn. *Diceros simus)*

Males often solitary. Several females may form a herd with a dominant bull. These herds of up to 10 are called a "laager".

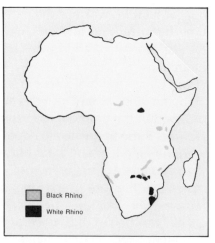

Black Rhino
White Rhino

	Male	Female
Height	6 ft	5⅓ ft
Weight	6600 lb	4400 lb
Weight at Birth	88 lb	88 lb
Age at Weaning	2 years	2 years
Age at Maturity	7 years	5 years
Gestation Period	—	18 months
Number of Young	—	1
Lifespan	45 years	45 years

BLACK RHINOCEROS *(Diceros bicornis)* Solitary. ENDANGERED SPECIES. .

	Male	Female			
Height	4⅔ ft	4 ft	Age at Maturity	7 years	5 years
Weight	3300 lb	2200 lb	Gestation Period	—	17 months
Weight at Birth	88 lb	77 lb	Number of Young	—	1
Age at Weaning	2 years	2 years	Lifespan	40 years	40 years

Identification Contrary to what their names would lead you to believe, both black and white rhinoceros have a slate-gray, very thick skin, heavily folded round the neck and are hairless except for the tip of the tail and the edges of the ears, which are fringed with thick bristles. The only variation in color comes from the mud or dust in which they've been wallowing.

The big difference between them is that the black rhino has a pointed, flexible upper lip which enables it to graze leaves and twigs — thus it is a *browser.* The white rhino has a square upper lip and grazes on grass. This results in their characteristic postures — the black moving with head held up and the white with it lowered. The white rhino also has a massive hump on its neck and is the larger of the two. In fact, next to the elephant, it is the largest living land mammal.

The horns are similar in both species and there is little apparent difference between male and female. The horns, grown by both sexes, consist of hair fused into a hard bone-like substance. A by-product of their horns is used as a medicine for rheumatism and was once used as a popular aphrodisiac in parts of Asia but the main use until recently was for traditional, ornate dagger handles worn by the men in Yemen. Consequently, the animals have long been hunted and are now endangered.

Habitat Open tree and bush savannah, thorn scrub and the lower slopes of mountains.

Habits Living mainly alone or in small family groups, the rhino is very territorial. Its home range always includes at least one waterhole, preferably with a mud-wallow. On the boundaries each male leaves dung-heaps at regular intervals. He visits these frequently to deposit more droppings which are scattered about with the hind legs and front horn to form a flattened patch, sometimes more than six feet (two metres) across. The probable reason for this is to warn other males that they are trespassing, and to advertise his own presence to single females who may thus be encouraged to enter his territory.

The two species of rhinoceros have different characters. The black rhino is short-tempered and will charge an intruder without much provocation. White rhinos are generally more docile, although they should still be treated with respect. Rhinoceros feed mainly in early morning and late afternoon and frequently drink at night.

Diet The white rhino eats grasses and the black rhino eats twigs and leaves.

Breeding There is no particular breeding season, and single offspring are produced at intervals of rarely less than three years.

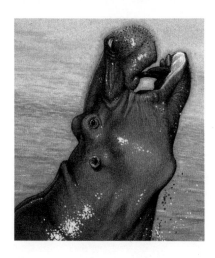

No Fish for the Hippo

(A Bushman story)

This is a story about why Hippo scatters his dung about. The story is common to most tribes of Africa, although it started with the Bushman.

When the Creator was giving each animal a place in the world, the pair of hippos begged to be allowed to live in the cool water which they so dearly loved.

The Creator looked at them, and was doubtful about letting them live in the water: their mouths were so large, their teeth so long and sharp, and their size and their appetites were so big, He was afraid that they would eat up all the fish. Besides, He had already granted the place to another predator — the crocodile. He couldn't have two kinds of large, hungry animals living in the rivers. So the Creator refused the hippos' request, and told them that they could live out on the open plains.

At this news, the two hippos began to weep and wail, making the most awful noise. They pleaded and pleaded with the Creator, who finally gave in. But He made the hippos promise that if they lived in the rivers, they must never harm a single fish. They were to eat grass instead. The Hippos promised solemnly, and rushed to the river, grunting with delight.

And to this day, hippos always scatter their dung on the river bank, so the Creator can see that it contains no fish bones. And you can still hear them laughing with joy that they were allowed to live in the rivers after all.

When Hippo was Hairy

(A Ndebele story)

The Ndebele have a story which explains why the hippo stays in the water all day and only comes out to feed at night. It goes like this:

Long, long ago hippos did not live in rivers and pools; they lived in the bush with other herd animals. In those days, Hippo had a very fine coat of glossy, chestnut-brown hair. He also had silky, soft ears and a beautiful bushy tail, of which he was overly proud.

Every day at noon when he had his drink, he would spend hours gazing at his own reflection in the water, turning this way and that to admire himself from every angle. His vanity was so great that he demanded that all the other animals should praise his beauty.

One day, when he was at the water's edge admiring his own reflection, he said to himself, "Oh, how handsome I am! Not a bit like that stupid Hare, with his coarse coat, long ears and silly twitchy nose. What a ridiculously short tail he has, and how clumsily he hops!"

Unfortunately for Hippo, Hare just happened to be nearby and he overheard what Hippo was saying. He was furious. He decided that Hippo needed to learn humility.

After thinking for a while, Hare collected a large pile of soft, dry grass under a large umbrella tree. He offered it to Hippo, saying, "O magnificent Hippo! Here is a warm bed that I have prepared for you, since winter is on its way and the nights are growing cold."

Hippo accepted the gift condescendingly and gave Hare a haughty nod. "Yes, Hare," he said, "I must be looked after. I am glad to see that you realize your responsibilities!"

Hare nearly choked with rage. What a vain creature Hippo was! "Just you wait, my fine friend," he thought to himself. And he helped Hippo to settle down comfortably.

Then Hare ran to a nearby village. While everyone in the village was busy drinking beer, he crept up to the cooking fire and stole some glowing embers. He carried them off on a piece of broken clay-pot.

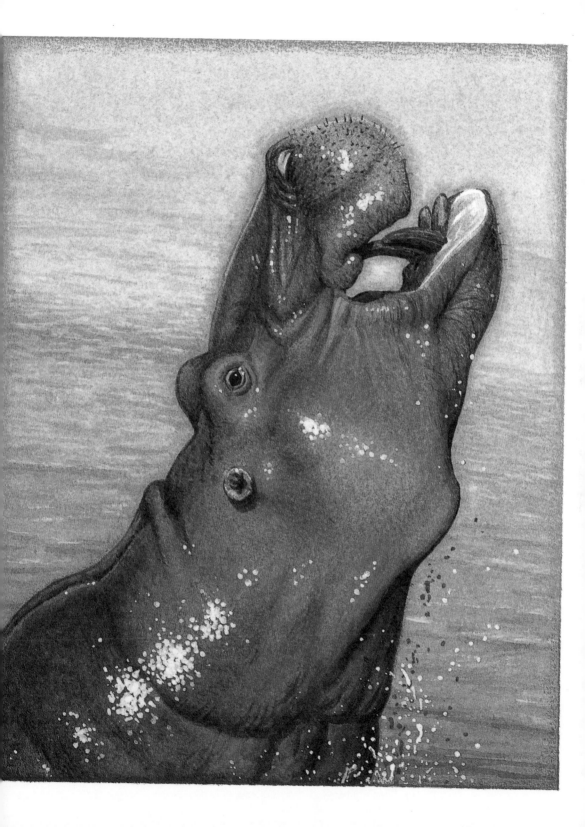

Hippo was snoring happily in his warm bed of dry grass when Hare got back. Hare crept up and threw in the burning embers, blowing on them until he had a fine blaze going. Poor Hippo awoke to find that his fine coat of fur was on fire! He heard Hare laughing nastily as he dashed off out of the way.

Hippo was confused and terrified, and at first he just thrashed about, trying to beat out the flames. Soon, however, the fire reached his skin, and in agony he charged away towards the waterhole. As he crashed through the bush, the fire spread to the dry winter grass and soon the whole area was ablaze.

Hippo reached the water just in time to save his life. The flames were put out and the cool water soothed his pain. The fire raged around the water's edge and Hippo had to hold his breath and sink beneath the surface. Only his eyes and nostrils showed when he came up for air.

The bushfire burned for a long time, but at last it died out. Hippo climbed out of the pool. He felt stiff, and sore, but he was very much alive. He

was going to find Hare and give him the beating of his life.

But Hippo couldn't resist his habit of pausing to look at himself in the pool. He got a terrible shock. Reflected in the water was a pinky-gray, wrinkled, bald creature. He could not believe his eyes. His lovely bushy tail was gone, all his hair had been burned off, and ugly, round, pink ears poked out where his long silky ones used to be. Without the fine glossy fur his legs looked short and stubby, and his flanks bulged with fat.

Hippo was horrified. He was ashamed, broken-hearted and, most of all, embarrassed. He rushed straight back into the water to hide his body from curious eyes. Weeping with shame at his dreadful appearance, he sank below the surface so that only his nostrils and eyes showed.

And there he has remained ever since. Hippo is now a creature of rivers and lakes. Only at night, when no one can see him, does he come out to walk and graze at the edge of the forest. Although he is still vain at heart, it happened so long ago that today hardly anyone remembers how Hippo once was hairy.

FACTS ABOUT HIPPOPOTAMUS

SPECIES:

HIPPOPOTAMUS *(Hippopotamus amphibius)*

Gregarious, living in herds of up to 20.

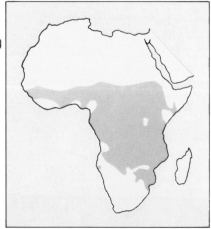

	Male	Female
Height	5 ft	4 ft
Weight	6600 lb	4400 lb
Weight at Birth	66 lb	66 lb
Age at Weaning	12 months	12 months
Age at Maturity	7 years	4 years
Gestation Period	—	8 months
Number of Young	—	1
Lifespan	30 years	30 years

Identification The hippopotamus is unmistakable: massive and ugly, with a very large head, wide squarish muzzle, "periscope" eyes, small ears, narrow nostrils which are closed under water, and short legs. Color varies from dark brown to grayish black, with pink around the eyes, sides of the face and underbelly.

Habitat Rivers, swamps and lakes bordered by vegetation.

Habits The name "hippopotamus" is derived from two Greek words meaning "horse" and "river." Hippopotamus spend most of their time in or close to water, during the day wallowing together in the shallows and backwaters or lying on sandbanks in the sun. At night they leave the water to graze and may travel far distances to find food. If alarmed they will bolt straight back to the water, scattering everything in their path, so it is unwise to get between them and the water!

They can stay beneath the water for 4 or 5 minutes at a time. If molested, they will raise just their nostrils above the water. Sometimes the whole head breaks the surface and water sprays about from the nostrils, accompanied by a roar-like bellow. Excellent swimmers, they can also walk well on the river or lake bed because of their weight. Consequently they play an important part in the ecology of river banks and swamps by keeping water channels open.

Diet Hippos are vegetarian, eating mostly grass and fine reeds which they crop very efficiently with their extremely hard lips.

Breeding Birth takes place on land, with usually a single calf. Hippos are good mothers, taking care to chase crocodiles away from the area where they keep their young, and teaching them to swim and wallow. They carry the very young calves on their backs in the water.

The Days of the Hunting Buffalo

(A Bushman story)

*In ancient Bushman lore, the buffalo was once a meat eater,
and a much-feared hunter.*

There was once a particular Buffalo, a huge and fierce bull who lived near the great swamps. He was a hunter of great strength and skill, and had a huge appetite which all the animals feared. So fierce was he that only the great Elephant and Rhino were safe from his deadly attacks.

One day, Buffalo caught Lion unawares while he was drinking at a pan. Buffalo was about to kill Lion with one sweep of his mighty horns, when Lion begged for mercy. Buffalo agreed to spare his life on one condition: that Lion would become his slave, and hunt food for Buffalo. Of course Lion agreed. What choice did he have?

So Buffalo commanded Lion to catch a fat springbok which was grazing on the other side of the pan. Lion obeyed, and dragged the prize back to Buffalo, who enjoyed a nice, easy meal. Buffalo thought to himself, "Well! This is a most excellent arrangement! I will now have time to enjoy my afternoon wallow, and sleep in the shade whenever I want!"

The next day, Buffalo called Lion again and ordered him to catch a tender young zebra, as he was hungry for his breakfast. Lion soon returned with

the catch and Buffalo greedily devoured the whole zebra. He didn't leave a scrap for Lion, not even a bone to reward him for his work.

After that, Buffalo found Lion every day and ordered him to kill more and more animals in order to satisfy his greed. Not once was there a morsel left for Lion.

Meanwhile, because their pride leader was spending all his time hunting for Buffalo, Lion's wives and cubs were beginning to find it difficult to hunt, and some of the cubs were starving. As the pride grew thinner and weaker, Buffalo grew fatter and greedier. After a while he was eating five times a day. Poor Lion wore himself out supplying food for dreadful Buffalo.

One day Buffalo found Lion lying wearily beneath a shady thorn tree. He ordered him to get up and prepare for a great hunt. Because of his easy life, Buffalo was now so huge and fat he could hardly walk. He had also developed a most astounding appetite.

"Today, Lion," said Buffalo, "you will go out and kill me one of every kind of animal in the bush!"

All at once, Lion knew that this was too much — an impossible task, especially as he was almost worn out. He protested: "O mighty one! Be reasonable! Even I could not manage such a thing." And he shook his great black mane in anger. "Do you not see my family? They are starving because I never have time to help them with the hunt. I beg of you, Great Buffalo, release me from my promise."

But Buffalo's greed was enormous, and he had no pity. "I spared your life!" he roared, "Now you must do my bidding if you value your honor!" And he pounded the ground with his enormous front hoof, raising a cloud of dust.

Lion drew himself wearily to his feet. He knew there was no longer any honor in the situation, and had decided to act.

"O Buffalo," he said, "regrettably, I am indeed honor bound to agree to your request. As you command me, through sheer greed, to kill one of every beast in the bush, I shall obey. And I will begin with you!"

So saying, Lion sprang onto Buffalo's enormous back and sank his great teeth into his neck, killing him immediately.

At last, Lion and his family had a huge feast, and after that they took a liking to buffalo meat, and continued to hunt for it whenever possible.

The other buffalo learned the lesson Lion had taught them, and started

to eat grass again. They also decided that it would be safer to live in herds, in order to protect themselves from the King of Beasts.

FACTS ABOUT BUFFALO
SPECIES:
BUFFALO *(Syncerus caffer)*

Males occur in small bachelor herds or are solitary.
Females occur in large herds of 100-1000.
Both sexes have horns.

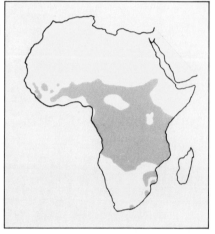

	Male	Female
Height	5⅓ ft	5 ft
Weight	1540 lb	1320 lb
Weight at Birth	88 lb	88 lb
Age at Weaning	12 months	12 months
Age at Maturity	8 years	4 years
Gestation Period	—	11 months
Number of Young	—	1
Lifespan	20 years	20 years

Identification Buffalo look massive, solid, indestructible, and in fact they are enormously strong. Their physique is the same as that of domestic cattle, except for slightly shorter legs and the huge blackish horns growing from a large, flattened, helmet-like plate covering and protecting the top of the head.

Habitat Buffalo can be found in a wide range of terrain, from the lower slopes of mountains to dense forests and open plains, but all habitats must have one feature in common — plenty of water, for buffalo must drink daily.

Habits Buffalo only have one persistent enemy, the lion, preying on the cows and calves and the old solitary bulls — which put up quite a fight! It is not unusual for lions to be killed or severely injured by the bulls. Occasionally buffalo will be taken by a crocodile, for they frequently swim rivers to reach lush vegetation on islands or far banks.

Like so many seemingly dangerous animals, if undisturbed buffalo are docile and harmless. If threatened or frightened, however, they can become fearsome adversaries, despite their relatively poor sight, which they make up for with excellent smell, hearing and cunning intelligence.

Diet Buffalo live mostly on grass and they particularly like the lush, sweet growth in river valleys. In times of drought they will browse on leaves and twigs.

Breeding There is no specific breeding time, though in some places it peaks during the July to September dry season.

The day Baboon outwitted Leopard

(A Zulu story)

Long, long ago, Baboon and Leopard were friends. One day, Leopard had chased Hare (you know why leopards chase hares now, don't you?), until Hare had taken refuge in an anthill. Leopard called her friend Baboon, and asked him to stand guard over the anthill while she went down to the river for a drink.

Baboon agreed, and settled down with his back to the side of the anthill, next to the hole where Hare had disappeared. It was a warm day, and fairly close to noon. After a while, Baboon started to doze off and was soon snoring gently.

Hare heard the snores and crept quietly out. As he was leaping away to safety, Leopard came back. She saw Hare disappearing over the hill and, in a rage, she charged up to sleeping Baboon and slapped him awake.

"O worthless monkey!" she roared. (This was a terrible insult, as baboons just hate being called "monkey.") "You have let that fine fat Hare escape. That's my lunch you have lost, you foolish ape!" And her eyes blazed in anger.

Now an angry, hungry leopard is not a very reassuring sight, and Baboon started to back away in fear. Leopard however, had not finished with him. She grabbed the frightened Baboon and was about to scold him even harder, when the feel of warm flesh between her paws suddenly made her stop in mid-sentence. Her eyes gleamed, and she licked her lips. "Hmm... As you have lost me my meal, I think you will do very nicely instead!" And, forgetting their past friendship, she opened her jaws to take a bite.

"Eee!" screamed Baboon. "Wait, O beautiful one! Let me at least pay for my crime in a proper manner. Did you not know, most lovely of beasts, that the best way to kill a baboon is to drop it from a height? We break into many small pieces, making an easy and tender meal for the hunter."

Leopard was amazed. She paused to think. But, seeing her hes'tate, Baboon chattered on, leaving her no time to reflect. "Just throw me up into this tree!" he jabbered, "You'll see — I will fall and split open just like a ripe calabash melon!"

Leopard couldn't resist the thought, so she tossed Baboon high into the branches above.

Quick as a flash, Baboon climbed up into the safety of the thickest thorns at the top. He started to laugh. He sat there screaming loud and long abuse at Leopard, calling her every name he could think of, and at the top of his voice. He even called her a mangy cat — and this made her yellow eyes blaze with rage. Other animals were beginning to gather around, attracted by the commotion. Leopard's pride could not stand it, and she bounded off, lashing her tail in fury.

But she never forgot the insults, and she never forgave them. To this day, the leopard hunts the baboon in preference to all other food. And the baboon screams with fear at the very sight of his deadliest enemy.

The Shona tribe of Zimbabwe have a superstition about the baboon. They believe that he is used by evil sorcerers as a "familiar", and can be a messenger. They think that people who are owed things pay the N'ganga (sorcerer) to send the baboon to collect the debt. The baboon then speaks in any language necessary. If the debt owed is in cattle, the baboon will not accept any excuses, and will spirit away the cattle without permission.

The magical powers that the baboon is thought to possess are probably due to the fact that he is so human-looking, but at the same time fierce and crafty.

FACTS ABOUT BABOONS
SPECIES:
CHACMA BABOON *(Papio ursinus)*
Gregarious; live in troops of 10-200.

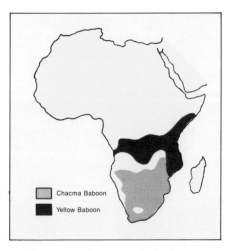

	Male	Female
Height	39 in	31 in
Weight	66 lb	40 lb
Weight at Birth	9 oz	9 oz
Age at Weaning	6 months	6 months
Age at Maturity	5 years	3 years
Gestation Period	—	6-7 months
Number of Young	—	1
Lifespan	25 years	25 years

Chacma Baboon

Yellow Baboon

Identification Baboons are easily distinguished from other monkeys because they are large, with a protruding, squarish muzzle, rather like most dogs. They are covered with a yellowish olive-brown coarse hair which is darker on the top of the head and along the spine and can be up to 1 ft in length.

Habitat Mostly in woodland, particularly in areas of rough country with rocky outcrops.

Habits These large, powerful, highly intelligent monkeys have an organized social life in troops ranging from 10-200 depending upon the availability of food.

Whether nesting, feeding or on the move, the dominant males, mothers and young stay in the center of the troop, while the weaker males, females without young and juveniles nearing maturity feed or play around them, acting as sentinels or as scouts.

It can be fascinating to watch a troop of baboons arrive at a waterhole to drink. The dominant males immediately climb trees or any other vantage point from which they can use their acutely developed eyesight to look for danger. If they see none, they remain silent, and the rest of the troop quickly approach the water. And if there are other animals waiting, such as antelope, which have been too nervous to drink, these will immediately follow the baboons to the water's edge and satisfy their thirst.

Diet Baboons are also like humans because, being omnivorous, they can eat meat, vegetation, fruit and indeed most chewable material. However, the bulk of their diet is vegetarian, mostly grass supplemented by seeds, shoots, tuberous roots and rhizomes which they dig up; buds, flowers, seed pods and fruits.

Breeding Within the troop, there is no family or "harem." When in season, the females present themselves first to the less dominant and then to the dominant males. They breed throughout the year.

Why Giraffe and the Oxpecker are Good Friends

(A Bushman legend)

In ancient times before the coming of man, when all the animals lived together peacefully, a huge bushfire swept through the land, started by a bolt of lightning. The tinder dry grass burst into flames and the strong winds that are common before the rainy season, quickly spread a wall of flames from horizon to horizon. Unable to do anything to put it out, the animals fled in panic before the deadly flames.

A pair of oxpeckers had made their nest in a hole in a tree trunk and had just hatched out their chicks, but the tree stood in the path of the advancing flames. The oxpeckers pleaded with the passing animals to help them rescue their little chicks, but they took no notice as they ran from the deadly flames.

Just when the desperate oxpeckers were about to give up hope, the kind giraffe came along and seeing the birds so distressed asked what was wrong. "Oh Giraffe," the oxpeckers wailed, "Our nest will soon be burned and our chicks with it. Please carry it away from the fire for us."

Giraffe took pity on the oxpeckers in their dreadful plight and rushed to the tree through the dense smoke and the flying sparks. Because of his long legs and neck, Giraffe was able to reach to the top of the tree

and pluck the nest and the young fledglings from the hole and carry them to safety.

"Oh, thank you, thank you, kind Giraffe," said the much relieved oxpeckers, "How can we ever repay you for your kindness?"

"That will be quite easy," replied the Giraffe, "I am always troubled by ticks. If you like you can ride on my back and pick the ticks off for me."

"We will gladly do this service for you for ever and ever," replied the overjoyed oxpeckers.

Today, if you go into the African bush you will nearly always see oxpeckers riding along on Giraffe, crawling over his neck, flanks and even into his ears, meticulously keeping their promise.

Why the Giraffe has a Long Neck

(An East African story)

In the beginning, the Creator gave Giraffe the same legs and neck as all the other animals; in fact Giraffe resembled some of the larger antelope such as Eland and Kudu.

All was well until one year a terrible drought afflicted the land. All the animals began to go hungry, as the best grazing and browsing were eaten. All that remained were the bitter tufts of yellowed turpentine grass and dry, shriveled twigs. There was great competition among the animals and they had to walk many weary miles each day between feeding areas and the few remaining waterholes. In times like these, only the fittest and strongest of the animals could survive.

One day, Giraffe met his friend Rhino out on the scorched plains where the dust-devils whirled and the horizon shimmered in the terrible heat. They trudged wearily along the trail back to the waterhole, and as they walked they complained about the hard times and the lack of food.

"Ah, my friend," said Giraffe, "See how there are too many animals searching out here on the plains — all they do is trample the remaining grass into the dust. And yet look at those tall acacia trees over there."

"OOMPHhh," said Rhino. (He wasn't — and still isn't — a very gifted talker.)

"How lovely it would be," continued Giraffe, "to be able to reach the topmost branches, where the tender green leaves are. Now there you have plenty of food, but I can't climb trees and I don't suppose you could either."

Rhino agreed, squinting nearsightedly up at the beautiful canopy of thick green leaves. "Perhaps," he said, "we could see the Man-Magician." He paused. "He's very wise and powerful." And he nibbled a dry twig, thinking.

"What a good idea!" said Giraffe, "Which way, old friend? Do you think he could help us?" And the two friends set off into the sunset, stopping on the way for a quick drink at the muddy waterhole.

After a long and tiring walk through the night and half-way through the next day, Rhino and Giraffe finally found the dwelling of the witchdoctor and explained their problem.

The Man-Magician laughed and said, "Oh, that is fairly easy. Come here tomorrow at noon and I will give you both a magic herb to eat. It will make your legs and your necks grow so long, that you will be able to reach the tree tops!"

The Man-Magician busied himself preparing his magic, and Giraffe and Rhino, both greatly excited, went back to the waterhole.

The next day, only Giraffe was at the witchdoctor's hut at the arranged time. Poor dimwitted Rhino had found a patch of nice green grass which had somehow escaped the notice of the other animals. And, quite forgetting about his noon appointment, he was greedily tucking into his unexpected meal.

After waiting for some time for Rhino to appear, the Man-Magician finally grew impatient. He gave Giraffe all of the magic herbs and disappeared into the shade of his hut. Giraffe ate them all up, and as soon as he had finished, he felt the strangest tingling feeling in his legs and neck. He blinked. The ground was getting further away! What a funny feeling!

Giraffe closed his eyes in half-fear, half-giddiness. Then he opened them again. Oh, how the world had changed! He was high up in the air, he could see for miles! He looked down at his long, long legs and his long, long neck, and smiled. The magic had worked wonderfully well. And there, level with his eyes and not two paces away, was the thick green canopy of a tall acacia tree.

Eventually Rhino remembered where he was supposed to be, and trotted hurriedly up to the witchdoctor's hut. He was too late. He saw the new tall, elegant giraffe browsing from the tree tops to his heart's content, free from the competition of all the other animals. When the Man-Magician told him that there was no magic herb left, Rhino lost his temper. Thinking that the Man-Magician had tricked him, he lowered his great sharp horn and charged, chasing him a long way into the bush.

Some say that to this day, Rhino is always very bad-tempered, and chases people whenever he is reminded of the Giraffe's greatest gift, his long, beautiful neck.

The Giraffe in the Sky

(An ancient Bushman legend)

At the very beginning of time, say the Bushmen, the Sun did not know its way around the heavens. Giraffe had a habit of staring curiously at everything, and so the Creator thought that it would be a good idea to give Giraffe the task of watching over the Sun, so that it didn't go astray.

Giraffe took his job very seriously. (Indeed, he was so good at it that the Sun never again took a wrong turn.) The Creator was very proud of Giraffe, and He decided to honor him. He rearranged a few stars so that they made a giraffe shape in the sky, and you can still see it to this day.

The Bushmen call the pattern Tutwa (Giraffe), and use it to guide them when they travel at night. English-speaking people call Tutwa the Southern Cross, and use it as a guide, too.

FACTS ABOUT GIRAFFES
SPECIES:
GIRAFFE *(Giraffa camelopardalis)*
Males mainly solitary; females form small, loose herds of up to 20.

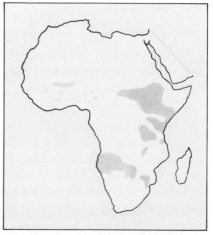

	Male	Female
Height (total)	18 ft	16 ft
Weight	2640 lb	1980 lb
Weight at Birth	220 lb	220 lb
Age at Weaning	6 months	6 months
Age at Maturity	5 years	4 years
Gestation Period	—	15 months
Number of Young	—	1
Lifespan	20 years	20 years

Identification No animal could be easier to identify than the giraffe, with its enormously long neck. It is the tallest animal in the world, reaching up to 18 feet (5.5 m). It has seven vertebrae in the neck, the same as other mammals, but they are very elongated. The two horns are really bony growths covered with skin and hair except at the tip. Both sexes have horns, and there is also a curious bony growth between the eyes. The coat varies somewhat in color and pattern but is generally reddish-brown in irregular patches divided by white to light fawn lines.

Habitat Giraffes live in open grassland country with light bush and acacia. They are never found in heavily forested country.

Habits The long neck, developed over countless thousands of years, enables the giraffe to browse on the topmost branches of the trees of the plains so that it does not have to compete with other browsing animals for food. This also enables the giraffe to see danger a long way off; other browsing and grazing animals therefore tend to stay close, using it as a sentinel. Any signs of nervousness from the giraffe and the others run off.

Its long slender legs allow it to run very fast — 30 miles per hour (50 km per hour) — and although the rather stiff-legged gait may seem ungainly at first sight, as the swaying rhythm develops, a galloping giraffe becomes a majestic sight. The legs are also the giraffe's only means of defense. It either kicks out brutally with the rear legs (and has been known to kill lions in this way), or rears up and chops down very hard with the sharp front hooves.

Giraffes are most vulnerable to attack when drinking, for they have to splay their legs right out in order to lower their heads to reach the water. It is difficult for them to get up quickly and lions quite often catch them in that position by leaping on their backs. When that happens, they have been observed galloping through thick bush in an attempt to knock the attacker off; their skin is extremely tough and remains unharmed by the thorns and branches. Generally, however, only young giraffes fall victim to lions.

Diet Giraffes browse on a wide variety of tall trees, eating leaves and shoots from the highest branches. As well as the long neck, they are aided by a long, prehensile upper lip and a tongue that can be extended some distance from the mouth. When water is available they drink frequently, but can live for long periods without it.

Breeding There is no special breeding season. Usually only one calf is born and starts to browse on its own at the relatively young age of a couple of weeks. Younger giraffes are left in a "nursery" group by day while their mothers go off to feed.

Why Waterbuck helped Crocodile

(A Makushu story from the Okavango)

Long ago, after the coming of man who brought hunting to the Earth, all the animals were afraid of Lion. He was the greatest hunter of all; even man was afraid of his strength and skills.

In these early days, Waterbuck lived in small herds and mixed with the other animals of the plains. When Lion was hunting, Waterbuck, like the other animals, would flee from him; none but mighty Elephant could hope to defend himself against such strength and ferocity. Lion was very fast and hunted together in prides so many animals, great and small, fell to the King of Beasts.

One day Waterbuck had to flee for his life when his herd was attacked by Lion, but after a long chase Waterbuck was lucky enough to escape. He had run such a long way he had left the plains behind and saw for the first time a vast area of swamps and forests. Wandering through the reed beds and huge forests of waterberry and fig trees, Waterbuck decided that this would be a good place to live; lots of food, plenty of water and, most important of all, plenty of cover to hide from Lion.

Suddenly Waterbuck heard wails and cries for help. Near the water's edge a huge crocodile had been trapped beneath a fallen branch and was unable to move. Seeing Waterbuck he called, "Please help me, I beg you. As you can see I am trapped and will surely die from starvation."

Now Waterbuck knew all about the sly, cunning Crocodile who was as feared a hunter of the waters as Lion was of the plains. Waterbuck felt pity for Crocodile and decided to help, but first he said, "For all your strength, O Great Scaly One, you will surely die should I walk away. Yet I will save you provided you agree to one condition."

"Name what you will, O Merciful One; for the gift of my life I am bound to honor your desire," pleaded Crocodile.

"In return for your life you will allow me to enter the water at will, whether to cool off in the summer heat or to escape from my enemies. You, Crocodile, must leave me in peace in your domain."

To this Crocodile gladly agreed, and Waterbuck set about freeing the huge reptile. Although the branch was thick and a great weight, Waterbuck managed to use his horns as a lever to pry the log up, allowing Crocodile to slither free.

As Crocodile was about to swim off Waterbuck said, "Remember your promise, Scaly One; I have proven my great strength to you. All would not go well with you should you break your word."

Crocodile vowed to keep his word and swam off, thanking Waterbuck for his kindness.

To this day when Waterbuck is chased by Lion he runs to the safety of water (most members of the cat family hate getting wet and do not chase prey into deep water). Waterbuck knows he is safe from attack by Crocodile, thanks to his act of kindness, and perhaps Crocodile is just a little bit scared of the strength of Waterbuck.

How the Waterbuck got its White Circle

One dark night, when there was no moon, a waterbuck mother and her young ones grazed very close to a tribesman's hut. This man had been busy whitewashing the walls of his hut in preparation for a visit by a relative, and he had left the pots of whitewash outside.

One of the waterbuck accidentally knocked over the pots in the dark, making such a noise that the tribesman woke up. He ran outside and was very angry to see that all of his nice white paint had been spilled. He shouted at the buck, and chased them. The waterbuck scattered and ran in all directions.

In his anger, the tribesman picked up a pot and threw it at the mother waterbuck. It struck her firmly on the hindquarters, and left a large white circle on her rump. Now this was very useful, because it showed up nicely in the dark, and her young ones were able to follow her to the safety of the forest.

When the waterbuck realized what a useful thing it was to have a white ring around their bottoms, they decided to keep it, and from that day to this, no self-respecting waterbuck has been without one.

FACTS ABOUT WATERBUCK
SPECIES:
COMMON WATERBUCK
(Kobus ellipsiprymus)
Found in small herds of up to 20. Only the male has horns.

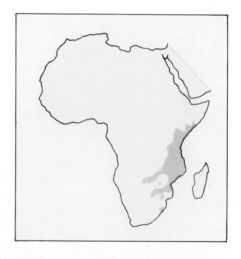

	Male	Female
Height	4⅓ ft	4 ft
Weight	550 lb	440 lb
Weight at Birth	18 lb	18 lb
Age at Weaning	9 months	9 months
Age at Maturity	2 years	2 years
Gestation Period	—	8 months
Number of Young	—	1
Lifespan	10 years	10 years

Identification Common waterbuck are big, strong-looking antelopes, the males carrying two long, heavily ringed horns angled backwards and sweeping gently out, up and finally becoming perpendicular. Coats are coarse, reddish or grayish-brown in color, with a shaggy mane around the neck of both male and female.

Very distinctive features are a white band round the tail on the buttocks and another encircling the throat from the base of each ear. This species is very similar to the defasa or sing sing waterbuck, except that the defasa has no ring and the inner sides of its buttocks and upper legs are white.

Habitat As the name suggests, waterbuck are usually found near water and where there is plenty of grass in tree- and bush-savannah areas.

Habits Waterbuck live in small herds of about 20 or so. Sometimes several herds will congregate together for short periods. Males have several females and fight off rivals with their magnificent, sweeping horns, which they also use to defend their families from predators. The males are not often attacked except by lions, but young bulls, calves and cows are the prey of cheetahs, leopards and wild dogs. To defend themselves, they frequently leap into the nearest water, submerging themselves with only their nostrils above the surface, the bulls using their great horns like scythes to beat off their attackers. They seem to have no fear of crocodiles and there is a theory that the strong smell coming from glands in their skin wards off crocodiles, although many experts say it serves only to keep off parasites and other biting insects.

Diet The bulk of a waterbuck's diet consists of grass and it particularly likes reedy growth on the edge of dams and swamps. It will also eat some bush leaves.

Breeding Young are born throughout the year, though some authorities say that September, October and November are the most common times. Multiple births are rare.

The First Zebra

(A tale from the Angoni of Central Africa)

In the beginning when all was new on the Earth the animals were all similar, none having special horns or colorful coats. The Creator was busy finishing off his great work and fashioned a multitude of horns of various sizes and shapes and coats of many types and colors. When He had finished He left them in a cave close to the shores of a great lake.

The Creator then sent a message to all the animals living on the grassy plains, that they should go to the cave the next morning and select the horns and coats they thought would suit them best. This caused a great flurry of excitement and anticipation and the animals were all eager to see what the Creator had made for them.

All, that is, except for Zebra, whose only concern in life was food, in fact it was well known among the other animals that Zebra was a glutton. When all the other animals moved off toward the lake at first light, Zebra did not join them. If he was going to take such a long walk he was going to have a good breakfast of luscious grass and he could not see why all the other animals were so carried away with the idea of horns and coats. Although the other animals urged him to hurry along to the cave, Zebra muttered that he would follow on in due course, when he had finished his breakfast. This was done through a mouthful of grass, so the other animals left the ill-mannered Zebra in disgust.

Several hours later Zebra decided he had had his fill, and slowly sauntered off towards the lake, following a broad trail left by the other animals. As

Zebra neared the lake, some of the animals were returning to the plains and Zebra was amazed by their change in appearance. Elephant had chosen a rather drab gray coat, but set this off with a magnificent pair of ivory tusks. Lion had chosen a sleek dusky coat with a regal mane of long black hair. Sable had a glossy black coat and vicious sweeping curved horns.

One by one Zebra passed all the animals in their brand-new finery. Finally, just as he was about to enter the cave, Zebra passed Rhinoceros. Unfortunately Rhino is very nearsighted; he had chosen a coat several sizes too large and it looked rather baggy on him. Also, he had chosen two horns

that were not the same size and stuck them on his nose. All in all, Rhino looked rather odd but he seemed very pleased with himself.

When Zebra went into the cave the only coat left was a boldly striped black-and-white one and he could find no horns at all. After such a long walk Zebra was feeling quite hungry again so he quickly tried on the remaining coat. This strange black-and-white coat did fit very well and as his belly was rumbling he did not care that it looked different; nor did he mind that no horns were left over for him.

Meanwhile, back on the plains, all the other animals were admiring each other in their brand-new finery. When Zebra got back to the plains he ignored all the others and just put his head down and started chomping away at his lunch. The other animals soon noticed the startling black-and-white coat and so they greeted Zebra with jeers and laughter.

"Look at the greedy Zebra in his funny new coat and without any horns!" cried the Duiker scornfully. Soon all the other animals had taken up the chorus.

Zebra did not care. What did horns matter when all that really counted was plenty of tender green grass to eat whenever he wanted? To this day Zebra has not needed any horns, but he is always fat and glossy in his peculiar black-and-white coat.

How the Zebra got his Stripes

(A Zulu story)

One day long ago, a very big, very fierce baboon came down from the trees to live on the banks of the great Umfolozi River. Here he made his home and declared to all the other animals that the land all around belonged to him, and they were not to use the water in the river. He alone was to be allowed to drink.

There was one among the animals who decided to stand up to fearful Baboon. This was a proud young zebra stallion, Dube.

In those days, zebras were pure white, like the fabled unicorn. Now Dube was brave, and he challenged Baboon to a fight. Baboon, a fierce veteran

of many battles, agreed. He knew all about fighting.

"The loser of the fight," he said, "will be banished forever to the barren kopje across the river." And he told the zebra to come to his kraal the next morning.

The fight was long and terrible. Both animals fought with all their strength, using the weapons the Creator had given them. Dube used his sharp hooves and teeth. Baboon used his long fangs and his agility.

Eventually, Baboon gained the upper hand, and poor Dube was thrown backwards into the blazing logs of the kraal fire. The cruel flames licked all over his body, searing his fine white coat. The dreadful pain gave Dube a surge of new strength, and with a mighty kick he sent Baboon flying. Over the river sailed Baboon, right onto the rocks of the kopje on the other side. Baboon landed with such force that a bald patch remains on his behind to this very day.

But Dube too was marked for life. The burns from the blazing logs in Baboon's fire left black stripes all over his snow-white coat. But at least he had won and from that day on, the water was free to all the animals.

Since then, zebras wear their stripes with pride, and while baboons are banished to stony kopjes, the zebras dwell on the open plains, coming and going to the river just as they please.

FACTS ABOUT ZEBRAS
SPECIES:
BURCHELL'S ZEBRA *(Equus burchelli)*
Gregarious, in small herds of up to 40.

	Male	Female
Height	4 ft	4 ft
Weight	704 lb	616 lb
Weight at Birth	66 lb	66 lb
Age at Weaning	11 months	11 months
Age at Maturity	3 years	3 years
Gestation Period	—	12 months
Number of Young	—	1
Lifespan	20 years	20 years

Identification The zebra is very much like a horse or large pony covered in black-and-white stripes. It is the wild horse of Africa. Although the markings appear the same from a distance, in fact every single zebra's stripes are different.

Habitat Lightly wooded and open grasslands near water.

Habits The zebra is an animal which prefers to run in herds of its own kind, living in groups of up to 40. The male (called a stallion, like a horse) gathers his own group of females around him and fiercely guards them from rivals. Fights between stallions can be heard a long way off; they make fierce noises, barks, and high-pitched whinnies as they rear at each other, kicking and biting with murderous intent.

Sometimes zebras mix with herds of blue wildebeest. The two species eat different types of grass, so they do not compete for food. Both need plenty of water and will travel long distances to get it.

Zebras are one of the lion's favorite prey animals. Their defense is to kick out viciously with their hind hooves. Many a lion has faced a miserable death through starvation because its jawbone has been broken by such a well-aimed kick.

The zebra is a cousin of the horse and the donkey, and its hoof prints and droppings are similar. You might think that its bold black-and-white stripes are the reverse of camouflage — as they are, close up. But at a distance, on the open plains when the heat shimmers up from the ground, the zebra's stripes seem to fade and blur until even a whole herd is almost invisible from a few miles away. The stripes can also be a means of confusing a predator as it moves in close to a running herd. Imagine trying to pick out any one particular zebra from a jumbled mass of moving black-and-white lines!

You will never see a thin-looking zebra because the body fat on a zebra is stored deeper inside the animal, not just under the skin. The only way to tell if a zebra is starving is when its mane starts to flop over to one side, because the one place where fat is stored near the surface, is along the ridge of the neck.

Zoologists have found that zebras actually form close "friendships" with one or two other animals in the herd, and these small groups of "friends" are always together.

Diet Zebras are grazers, but in hard times when grass is scarce they will dig up roots with their front hooves and eat them.

Breeding There is no particular breeding season. Foals are born singly and, amazingly, within a matter of hours from birth, can keep up with the rest of the herd.

How Tsessebe got his Peculiar Horns

(A Bushman story)

Right at the beginning of time, when the Creator, with the help of the great Mantis, was making all the animals, he was faced with an enormous task. There was so much work to do that when He was getting near the end, He was tired and so hurried to finish. In fact, He was in such a rush that He forgot to give Tsessebe any horns!

All the other bucks made fun of poor Tsessebe. Their own heads were proudly decorated with a variety of horns, all different shapes and sizes, but all handsome, graceful and very useful.

Tsessebe was miserable. He wandered alone for a long time, wondering why he had been left out. He avoided contact with the antelopes and gazelles since they would laugh at him. Eventually, he plucked up his courage. He decided that he would go back to the Creator and beg to be given some horns.

The Creator was resting after his great work, and was annoyed at being disturbed. He listened to Tsessebe, and became angry that the mistake should be drawn to His attention.

When Tsessebe had finished his plea, he hung his head and waited. The Creator impatiently grabbed a few twisted old leftover bones, and stuck them on the buck's head.

"Now let's hope you are satisfied!" He said, and sent Tsessebe away.

When the other animals saw Tsessebe's new horns, they made more fun of him than ever. Tsessebe did look very odd — and as their laughter rang out, he was even more miserable.

Being a timid and gentle creature, he did not dare to go back to the Creator again. He decided, sadly, that he would have to be content with what he had; after all, even funny-looking horns were better than no horns at all.

However, the Creator heard the mocking shouts and laughter, and seeing Tsessebe's plight, He took pity and relented. He made Tsessebe a present and gave him the magnificent gifts of speed and agility.

At last, all the other antelope began to envy Tsessebe. Now he runs like the wind and doesn't mind about his horns at all.

FACTS ABOUT TSESSEBE
SPECIES:
TSESSEBE or SASSABY *(Damaliscus lunatus lunatus)*
Gregarious, in small herds of up to 20.
ENDANGERED SPECIES

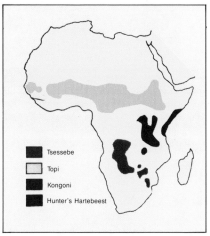

	Male	Female
Height	4 ft	4 ft
Weight	352 lb	319 lb
Weight at Birth	22 lb	22 lb
Age at Weaning	6 months	6 months
Age at Maturity	4 years	3 years
Gestation Period	—	8 months
Number of Young	—	1
Lifespan	12 years	12 years

Map legend:
- Tsessebe
- Topi
- Kongoni
- Hunter's Hartebeest

Identification Tsessebe is one of the larger antelopes, with a long face, sloping back and humped shoulders. The horns are crescent-shaped with very pronounced rings. Color is purplish chocolate-brown, with bare patches beneath the eyes and dark gray-black smudges on thighs and shoulders. Both sexes have horns.

Habitat Open grasslands and swampy floodplains.

Habits The tsessebe is the fastest antelope in southern Africa. It can outrun all but the swiftest of predators, and has been clocked at 37 miles per hour (60 km per hour) — as fast as a top racehorse. Tsessebe are normally found near wildebeest and zebra and, like them, prefer open areas. They are also herd animals, like their cousin the wildebeest. Tsessebe have the peculiar habit of standing stock-still on top of anthills for a long time. They do this to show other tsessebe that this territory belongs to them. It probably also helps them to look out for predators.

Diet They graze almost entirely on grass.

Breeding Calves are usually born singly in September and October.

Why the Wart Hog goes about on his Knees

(A Zulu story)

Wart hog had made himself a lovely, spacious home in an old anteater hole. He had built it up and made a wide entrance, and thought it was quite the grandest hole in the area. But one day Wart hog looked out and was horrified to see a lion stalking stealthily towards his cave.

Thinking quickly, he pretended to be supporting the roof of his hole with his strong back, pushing up with his tusks. "Help!" he cried to the lion, "I am going to be crushed! The roof is caving in! Perhaps you had better flee, O Lion!"

However, the lion had been caught out once before with a trick like this (remember sly old Jackal?), and he was not going to be fooled a second time. He roared so fiercely that Wart hog dropped to his knees, trembling, and begged for mercy. Luckily for him, Lion was not really all that hungry. Also, he was amused to think the slow-witted wart hog would try to copy Jackal's trick. So he pardoned the wart hog and left, saying, "Stay on your knees, you foolish beast!"

Wart hog took this to be an order and that is why, even today, you will see Wart hog feeding on his knees, in a very undignified position, with his bottom up in the air and his snout snuffling in the dust.

Why Wart Hog Is So Ugly

(A story from East Africa)

In the beginning, Wart hog was a small but handsome beast. Unfortunately he was also despised by all the other inhabitants of the savannah because he was vain and rude. Even Hare could not tolerate Wart hog's superior attitude.

One thing Wart Hog had learned from the start was how to make himself a comfortable home. These were usually old aardvark holes, no longer required by the original owner, and with some alteration and enlarging they were ideal.

In this snug, comfortable home he was safe from prowling hunters at night, and during the day he never ventured too far from safety. This retreat was needed quite frequently because Wart hog's rudeness meant that he was often scurrying to safety.

Bright and early one morning Wart hog was out enjoying a meal. He was feeding on roots and grass shoots with his bottom sticking up in the air in a most undignified manner, so busy eating that he failed to notice Porcupine.

After a night of walking around searching for food Porcupine was exhausted and, seeing an inviting-looking hole, quickly scurried down the passage and was soon curled up in the main chamber of Wart hog's hole, sound asleep.

After several hours of feeding, Wart hog trotted off to the nearby waterhole and had a good wallow in the mud. Feeling much refreshed, he was about to head off to find more grazing when he noticed Lion strolling by. Unable to resist the temptation Wart hog passed some very rude remarks about Lion's mane looking very messy and unkempt. This was too much for Lion, who had far too many tricks played on him, and too many undignified remarks from such a rude little fellow. So Lion charged Wart hog, hoping to catch him and teach him a lesson that he would never forget.

Seeing the enraged Lion bearing down on him, Wart hog was seized by panic and sprinted off towards his den. A great chase ensued, but eventually Wart hog arrived safely at his home and shot down the tunnel. Lion was left to stand guard at the top.

Meanwhile, Porcupine, who had been fast asleep, woke with a start, sure that some predator had found her down the hole and was coming to grab her. Jumping to her feet, Porcupine braced herself for an attack, spreading out her long, sharp quills. Wart hog, unable to stop, came bursting through into the chamber, straight into Porcupine. Wart hog got a face full of sharp, painful quills.

Lion was startled to hear a great yelp of pain come from Wart hog's den. There was the sound of a considerable commotion from under the ground and then Wart hog shot out of the tunnel, screaming and howling in pain. He had a dozen or so quills sticking out of his cheeks, nose and forehead, plus the signs of a great many more puncture holes.

Lion saw and heard the obvious discomfort of Wart hog and decided that he might have learned his lesson and so left him to his pain.

Wart hog was most miserable, especially as none of the animals would help him pull out the quills, remembering how rude and vain he had been in the past. Wart hog's face swelled up and was sore for a very long time.

To this day Wart hog is covered in warts and bumps and he is no longer handsome. Taught his lesson, he is now a humble animal who minds his own business. As if reminded of his painful experience, Wart hog now enters his den backwards to protect his face from further damage.

FACTS ABOUT WART HOGS
SPECIES:
WART HOG *(Phacochoerus aethiopicus)*
Found in pairs and small family groups.

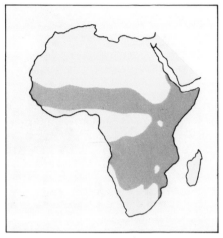

	Male	Female
Height	29 in	28 in
Weight	154 lb	132 lb
Weight at Birth	1¾ lb	1¾ lb
Age at Weaning	3 months	3 months
Age at Maturity	2 years	14 months
Gestation Period	—	4½ months
Number of Young	—	3-7
Lifespan	12 years	12 years

Identification There is no mistaking the wart hog with its curved upper tusks, large ugly facial "warts" and gray body. It is hairless except for the bristles on the cheeks and shoulders, dark erect mane and bristly tail tip. Both sexes have tusks.

Habitat They live near water in open tree- and shrub-grasslands.

Habits Living in small family groups (mother, father and young), they are frequently seen because, unlike many other animals, they drink during the day, often when the sun is at its highest. They frequently use abandoned anteater holes and other burrows as lairs toward which they will bolt when frightened, holding their thin tails upright like radar antennae presenting a most amusing sight. They enter the lair backwards, so their sharp tusks face out and can be used to fend off attacking animals.

Their main enemies are lions, leopards, cheetahs, hyenas and packs of wild dogs.

Like domestic pigs, they have poor eyesight but an excellent sense of smell and hearing. Despite their ferocious appearance wart hogs are not really aggressive unless cornered.

Diet They are grazers and root-eaters, feeding mostly on short grass and whole plants, roots and all. They have a habit of shuffling along on their front knees when foraging.

Breeding The average wart hog litter consists of three or four piglets, although up to eight have been observed.

The Race that was Rigged

(A Swazi story)

Tortoise was eating peacefully one day, minding his own business, when along came Mofuli, the hare. Mofuli, like all wicked little hares, could not resist the chance to make fun of Tortoise and tease him about how slow and ponderous he was.

Mofuli, full of mischief, challenged Tortoise to a race. There were some palm trees about 550 yards (500 metres) from where they were, and Mofuli said that was where they would race to.

Tortoise had had enough of Mofuli, and all hares, to last him a lifetime, since this was not the first time he had been teased by one of these irritating creatures. He wished he could put Hare in his place once and for all.

He thought for a moment and then said, "Speed is not everything, Mofuli. One must have endurance, too. Let us make this a real race — a long one. Let us race to the Blue Pan, some six miles (ten kilometres) from here. And, so that I have time to prepare, let us run the race in five days' time, at noon."

Mofuli was most surprised. He hadn't expected Tortoise to accept the challenge, and had been looking forward to a good long teasing. But he was scornful, and he almost decided not to bother with the race. But Tortoise was so much in earnest, that in the end he agreed. And Hare went on his way, laughing. He could hardly wait to tell all the other animals about the silly old Tortoise.

But Tortoise lost no time. He called on his relatives for help, telling them about his plan. It was very simple: at noon on Saturday, they were to place themselves in different positions all along the path that Hare and Tortoise were to race. Every one of them was to run toward Blue Pan, starting from different points along the route. All they had to do was to keep going as fast as they could, until Hare had sped past, and then they could go home and rest if they wanted to.

Tortoise collected a gourd to hold water, and set off for the pan that very day. It took him almost five days to get to Blue Pan, but at last he arrived. At noon on Saturday, he filled his gourd with water and settled down to wait.

Meanwhile, Mofuli had arrived at the starting point at the agreed time, and there he found Tortoise's cousin. It did not occur to Mofuli that this was a different tortoise. They greeted each other, and the race began.

Mofuli was out of sight in a twinkling, and Tortoise's cousin plodded off on his way, chuckling to himself. Mofuli was laughing too, until he reached the first rise and there was Tortoise ahead of him! (Actually, it was Tortoise's brother, stumbling along as fast as he could go.) Mofuli ran faster and soon he was out of sight. He was rather puzzled, and as the race went on, he became more and more confused.

Over each hill, Mofuli found Tortoise in front of him. Each time he overtook him, running like the wind, Tortoise would laugh loudly. By now, Hare was thinking that Tortoise must have learned to fly.

It was very hot, being midday, and the sun beat down. The pan was still two miles (three kilometres) away, and Mofuli was terribly thirsty. He came over the next rise to find Tortoise, ahead of him again!

In desperation, Mofuli put on his last burst of speed. Heart pounding, he strained every muscle, and at last came in sight of the Blue Pan. He was almost at the pan, when suddenly he tripped and fell. He lay on the ground, exhausted — he could go no further. His sides were heaving and every limb was trembling.

After a few moments he staggered to his feet. He looked up and what do you think he saw?

Why, Tortoise, of course, walking towards him from the pan, carrying a gourd of cool, clear water. This sight was more than Mofuli could stand. He fainted from shock and exhaustion.

Tortoise revived Hare by sprinkling cold water over his face. When Mofuli came round, Tortoise said in a soothing voice, "Drink this, my poor friend. I had an idea that you might be needing it. The endurance of some animals is not quite what they claim it to be." And he chuckled quietly to himself.

So it was that slow old Tortoise beat Hare at his own game. Clever as he was, Mofuli did not have the brains to see that he himself had at last been made a fool of.

The Tug-of-War

(A Ndebele story)

One peaceful morning a hare called Umvundla, who lived by the Zambezi River, was bored. He felt like creating a bit of fun for himself, so he looked around to see what he could do. Suddenly, he spotted two dignified old residents of the area — Rhino and Hippo.

Now Hippo, although aware of his ugliness, was very proud of his strength. Umvundla hopped up to the river bank and called: "O mighty one! Why do you say you are so strong? Even I, with my small size and thin legs, could beat you in a tug-of-war!"

Hippo ignored Hare with his ridiculous boasting. But Umvundla kept pestering him.

At last Hippo replied, in the hope of getting some peace and quiet, "A tug-of-war? All right, I will show you, my little long-eared nuisance."

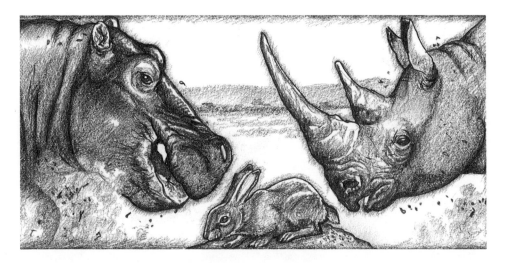

Umvundla danced with delight. He pointed to an old, rounded dome of earth beyond the river bank. "I bet I could pull you clear out of the water and over that termite hill," he taunted.

Umvundla then dashed off to braid a long, strong rope. When he came back, he tied one end to Hippo's hind leg, saying, "When I shout, 'Pull', from behind the hill you must pull with all your might, for I shall surely beat you!"

Hippo thought that Umvundla's foolishness had at last got the better of him. He said nothing, and settled down again in the water. In the warm shallows, he soon dozed off.

Now Umvundla took the other end of the rope, and crept around to the other side of the hill, where he knew that old bull Rhino was asleep in the shade. He picked up some fierce little red ants from a nearby hole and quietly dropped them in Rhino's ear. Rhino awoke with a grunt, and shook his head, trying to scratch his ears.

"Good morning!" piped Umvundla, "I was just coming to warn you of the ant's nest. Oh, I see one has crawled into your ear — may I help you to remove it? And with a great pretence of concern, he actually pushed the ants in further.

"That was most kind of you," said the unsuspecting Rhino, "Your small feet are just right, while mine are far too large for the job. You've no idea what trouble I have with ants." And on he grumbled, in the way of cranky old men everywhere.

"Well!" replied the cheeky Umvundla, "My feet may be small, but they are very strong. Stronger than yours, in fact. I'll show you just how strong I really am. I challenge you to a tug-of-war! I bet I can pull you right over this anthill and into the river!"

Old Rhino snorted with laughter. But at last he, too, was pestered into playing Umvundla's game. So Hare tied the other end of his rope around Rhino's hind leg. Then he hurried to the top of the hill. He hid in a little hollow, and called loudly, "PULL!"

As he shouted, the ants began to bite deep inside Rhino's ear, and with a bellow of pain, Rhino charged off.

Poor old Hippo had forgotton about Umvundla. He was dozing peacefully in his pool when there was a sudden, hard tug on his hind leg. Before he knew it, he was dragged out of the river and halfway up the hill.

When Hippo realized what was happening, he dug in his heels and gave a mighty heave, and the great tug-of-war started in earnest.

Each of the powerful animals strained with every muscle, and worked themselves up into a fine fury. Umvundla laughed so much that he fell over and went rolling down the side of the anthill. When they saw him, the two great animals knew they had been tricked.

Roaring with anger, they charged after Umvundla, hoping to trample him into the dust before he could tell the other animals how foolish they had been.

As they charged, the hare waited until the last possible moment, and then skipped out of the way. Hippo and Rhino were going so fast they couldn't stop. With a tremendous crash, they met head-on, hurting each other terribly. In a blind rage, they started to fight each other — until they heard Umvundla, who by this time was weeping with laughter.

Umvundla realized that at last the game was up, so he jumped up and sped off into the bush. He could hardly wait to tell the other animals how he had made fools of Hippo and Rhino.

To this day, Rhino thinks the little red ants are still in his ears. (Some say that the ants are so far down that they live in his brain, and this is why Rhino is so bad-tempered.)

As for Hippo, you will find him still searching the river banks at night, hoping to find Umvundla and throw him to the hungry crocodiles.

FACTS ABOUT HARES
SPECIES:
SCRUB HARE (Lepus saxatilis)
Solitary.

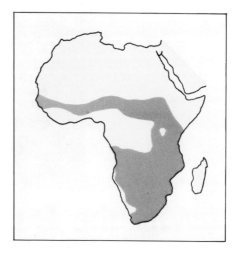

	Male	Female
Height	6 in	6 in
Weight	5½ lb	4¼ lb
Weight at Birth	¼ lb	¼ lb
Age at Weaning	1 month	1 month
Age at Maturity	8 months	8 months
Gestation Period	—	1 month
Number of Young	—	usually 2
Lifespan	5 years	5 years

Identification Very similar to the hares of Europe, America and other parts of the world. The scrub hare is one of many species common in Africa. It has long ears, strong hind legs which are longer than the front ones, and a white tail with a thick black stripe down the middle.

Habitat Dry, open country and sparse woodlands.

Habits The hare is usually nocturnal, hiding during the day in thick scrub or grass.

The hare is grass-colored and, by lying very still, avoids being noticed. However, if you are about to step upon a hare it will suddenly burst out from cover and run, zigzagging, until it is out of sight; this makes it very difficult to catch. Hares are preyed upon by eagles, owls, pythons and many other animals; including cheetahs, which are the only animals fast enough to run a hare down. Other hunters have to creep up close and make a surprise attack.

In African folklore, the hare is often the star of the story. He is portrayed as a creature who is always playing pranks and causing mischief. He is a boaster, always saying how clever he is, especially at making the high-and-mighty animals look silly. Hare always seems to come out on top!

Diet Hares feed on a variety of grasses, from which they also get enough moisture and so don't need to live near water.

Breeding Mother hares usually bear only two young at a time. Unlike rabbits, they do not live in holes, but make a shallow nest in the middle of a thick clump of grass, where the babies are left, keeping as still as stones, while the mother is out feeding.

Why the Dassie has no Tail

(A Xhosa fable)

Long ago at the dawn of time, and long before man appeared, the Lion was the King of all the animals, and furthermore, he was the only one to possess a tail.

Now, although he was very proud of the honor bestowed upon him by the Creator, he felt that his subjects should also have tails, as tails were so useful — and also because then Lion himself would not be such an odd man out. He made up his mind to make some tails himself, and give them to his subjects.

So, setting to work, he made tails of all shapes, sizes and colors. When he had finished, he told Baboon to call all the animals together, so that they might choose for themselves. Baboon was told to bring them all to Lion's Council Rock, and to make sure he forgot no one.

Baboon set off to call all, far and wide, and by nightfall they had started to assemble at the Council Rock. All, that is, except the lazy little Dassie. He felt that it was much too far to go. However, Dassie asked some passing monkeys to collect his present for him, and to explain to the King that he felt too ashamed to appear before Lion, as he was so small and humble. Satisfied that his message would be passed on safely, Dassie turned back into his cave and continued with his nap.

The old King Lion handed out tails to all the assembled animals, passing them over as each animal pointed to the one he had chosen. But Lion

made many mistakes due to his failing eyesight, in spite of a full, bright moon. (That is why, today, the squirrel has a tail much longer than his own body, while the elephant has such an embarrassingly short, thin tail.)

When most of the tails had been handed out, Lion noticed that Dassie was missing. The animals were all busy congratulating each other and comparing tails, when finally the monkeys, chattering noisily, remembered to pass on the Dassie's message. The King was very angry at the Dassie for disobeying the summons, but eventually he relented and picked out a small, furry tail for the monkeys to take back for Dassie. For after all, the King wanted all the animals to have a tail.

However, on their way back, the monkeys decided to teach the lazy Dassie a lesson, for they thought that Dassie did not deserve his present. So they stuck the little furry tail on to the end of their own brand new, long tails. They were rather pleased with the result.

On reaching Dassie's rocky home in a kopje, the monkeys showed off their gifts, parading about this way and that. They told the lazy Dassie what they had done to teach him a lesson. In future, they said, the Dassie was to obey the King, and stop being so idle.

Poor Dassie was most upset — but was far too lazy to do anything about it. So that is why, to this day, the dassie still has no tail.

FACTS ABOUT DASSIES
SPECIES:
DASSIE or ROCK HYRAX *(Procavia capensis)*
Gregarious, living in colonies of up to 200.

	Male	Female
Height	8 in	8 in
Weight	8¾ lb	6⅔ lb
Weight at Birth	½ lb	⅜ lb
Age at Weaning	4 months	4 months
Age at Maturity	12 months	12 months
Gestation Period	—	7½ months
Number of Young	—	2 or 3
Lifespan	7 years	7 years

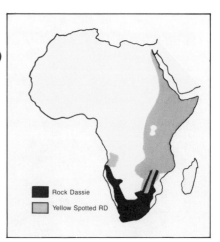

Rock Dassie
Yellow Spotted RD

Identification Plumpish little animals with a rounded head and small ears, short legs, no visible tail and a thick furry coat. Also known as rock rabbits, they are about the size of a large rabbit. However, unlike rabbits they are not rodents but are considered to be more closely related to the elephant!

Habitat Dassies live in colonies, and are always found among caves and crevices in kopjes or rock outcrops.

Habits Small, stiff hairs cover the pads of the dassie's feet, enabling it to scamper across smooth rock faces or along the branches of trees, without falling.

Dassies make a noise like a shrill bark or howl, and their alarm call is a whistle to warn others in the colony of approaching danger. They retreat into cracks and small caves where it is difficult for a predator to reach them.

Dassies are preyed upon by leopards, black eagles, pythons and other animals. Where there is human habitation, the dassies are usually in danger, for their fur pelts are greatly prized for use as warm winter blankets or kaross.

Diet Although dassies have very long front fangs, they are vegetarian, feeding on leaves, grass, fruit and twigs. The fangs are their only weapon of defense and can give a very nasty bite.

Breeding A mother dassie usually only produces two babies a year, so they cannot keep up numbers in their colonies as fast as rabbits.

The Foolishness of the Ostrich

(A Bushman legend)

At the beginning of time, Mantis (the Creator's assistant) was doubtful about giving fire to the world. He was afraid that any being that had the use of fire might destroy himself with it. So he decided to give Ostrich the job of guarding fire so that no one could play with it. He thought to himself, "If any being can get the fire away from loyal and stubborn Ostrich, then they are obviously clever enough to use the fire wisely." And, satisfied with this arrangement, he gave Ostrich his strictest instructions and returned to the heavens.

Ostrich kept the fire well-hidden under one of his wings, but the first Bushman discovered where he was keeping it. The Bushman wanted the fire; he wanted it to cook his food with, to keep him warm at night, and to keep away the nighttime predators. How fine it would be for him and his family to have some fire! So the Bushman decided to make a plan to steal away the fire from Ostrich.

The next day, the Bushman, who even then could talk to the animals, went up to Ostrich and greeted him politely. Ostrich stared at him suspiciously, but returned the greeting.

"O fine and wise Ostrich," said the Bushman, "O greatest of all the birds. I have good news for you!"

"Oh yes?" said Ostrich, interested.

"Indeed, magnificent one," replied the Bushman, "I had a wonderful dream last night. I dreamed that you could fly!"

Ostrich looked annoyed. "How so?" he demanded.

"I dreamed that you would be given the gift of flight if you stood with wings outstretched in the strong wind before dawn. The dream told me that if you kept your eyes closed and wings out, you would then take off and soar like an eagle!"

Ostrich couldn't resist the thought of being able to fly. It was his dearest wish. And so the very next day, at dawn he stood high on a hilltop in the chill dawn wind, wings outstretched and eyes squeezed shut.

While he stood there, the Bushman crept up and snatched the fire from its hiding place, and made off as fast as he could.

Thus was man given the greatest gift of all from Mantis.

Ostrich was so upset at losing the fire, and from the disappointment of not being able to fly, that he became feeble-minded. In fact, he became such a silly bird that now he has to leave one or two eggs outside the nest while he is sitting on them, to remind him what he is supposed to be doing!

Why Ostrich has a Long Neck

(A Sesotho story)

Once upon a time Ostrich had a normal-sized neck, just like other birds. In those days, Ostrich and Crocodile were friends. All the other animals warned Ostrich that Crocodile was an evil animal, and not to be trusted. But Ostrich, for such a big bird, has a small head and few brains, so he took no notice.

One day Crocodile was very hungry, as he hadn't eaten for several days. None of the animals had dared to come near his pan, for fear of being caught and dragged into the water.

So Crocodile said to Ostrich, "My dear friend, a tooth of mine is aching. I have so many teeth — there always seems to be something wrong with one of them. Please put your head inside my mouth and see if you can tell me which one it is." And he opened his jaws, wide.

Foolish Ostrich did as he was asked, and wicked Crocodile closed his mouth on the bird's head. Then Crocodile started to pull backwards, into the water, where Ostrich would drown and thus make a fine meal for him.

But Ostrich, although stupid, was a large bird and very strong. He did not want to die, and so he pulled in the opposite direction.

Both were equally determined to win this fight, and as they pulled and pulled, Ostrich's neck started to stretch and stretch. It grew longer and longer, and must have been very painful for poor old Ostrich, but he did not give in.

At last Crocodile got tired and let go. Poor Ostrich ran away, and ever since then he has lived in sandy places, far away from rivers. He still has a long neck and he never, never goes near crocodiles.

The Ostrich and her Chicks

(A tale from the Masai)

Long ago a pair of ostriches, having laid a large clutch of eggs, hatched them, and started to rear them.

Soon after, a passing lion noticed the chicks while they were left unattended by their parents, and so took them. Lion hid them in his den, intending to eat them one by one. Finding her chicks gone Ostrich followed their tracks to Lion's den and demanded her chicks back, but Lion refused and chased her away.

Ostrich went to the Council of Elders and pleaded for their help, but they were afraid of Lion and decided that the chicks were the Lion's children. Very much disappointed, Ostrich called a meeting of the other animals to be held at a large ant heap in front of Lion's den. At this ant heap Mongoose lived in a hole he had dug himself, which had two exits.

When all the animals had collected at the ant heap they too became afraid of Lion and agreed that the chicks were Lion's children. At this point Mongoose spoke out, saying, "Well, I for one have never seen an animal with hairs have young with feathers. Think what you may, the chicks belong to Ostrich!"

Lion was furious to have a mere mongoose challenge his authority and leapt at Mongoose, intending to kill him as an example to the other animals. Mongoose was too quick for Lion, however, and jumped down his hole in the ant heap. Safe from Lion, he ran through his tunnels and escaped out of the other hole, which Lion did not know about.

The enraged lion stood guard over the hole and, although he grew hungry Lion did not dare go away for fear that Mongoose would escape. Not only did he still believe that Mongoose was trapped underground, but he still wanted to teach the other animals a lesson they would never forget.

Lion was so determined he did not leave his post for several days until he fainted from hunger and fatigue. At last Ostrich was able to run into Lion's den and rescue her chicks. She was eternally grateful to the cunning little mongoose.

Mind you, to this day Ostrich is still very forgetful and her chicks have to be able to look after themselves soon after hatching.

FACTS ABOUT OSTRICHES
SPECIES:
OSTRICH (Struthio camelus)

Usually in pairs. Young are gregarious.

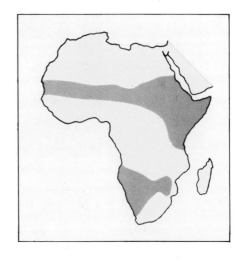

	Male	Female
Height	6¾ ft	6 ft
Weight	308 lb	264 lb
Weight at Hatching	3⅓ lb	3⅓ lb
Age at Maturity	8 years	8 years
Incubation Period	45 days — incubation shared	
Number of Eggs	—	12-20
Lifespan	50 years	50 years

Identification The ostrich is the largest bird on earth. Standing tall on long, bare legs, it also has a long, curving, predominantly white neck. The humped body of the male is covered in black patches and the wings and tail are tipped with white. The female is brown and white. Ostriches are flightless but can run very fast — up to 44 miles per hour (70 km per hour).

Habitat The ostrich is found in many of the drier areas of Africa.

Habits Ostriches are preyed upon by lions and cheetahs, and many smaller predators also eat the chicks and eggs if they get a chance. The chicks, however, have very good camouflage, and are able to run quite fast soon after hatching.

The adults use their powerful legs not only to run fast to escape enemies, but as weapons to keep attackers at bay. They tend to live in small, scattered groups or sometimes singly.

Diet Ostriches are mainly vegetarian, eating grass, succulents, berries and seeds, though they will also eat insects. They swallow large numbers of pebbles which help grind the harder food in the gizzard.

Breeding Ostriches normally mate for life, and they share the task of incubating the eggs. The male, which has mostly black feathers, sits on the eggs at night, and the drab, brown female covers them during the day. In this way, the nest is much harder to see.

The female does not make a nest of any sort, laying up to 20 eggs in a bare, shallow dip in the ground. Once the young ones hatch, it is usually the male ostrich which looks after the chicks until they are old enough to fend for themselves.

The Living Stones

(A Swazi legend)

The Creator, who made all the animals, also made a pair of creatures known as living stones, because they looked so much like a pair of cracked, brown rocks. These were, of course, Tortoise and his wife.

The Tortoises lived together for many, many years. But to their sorrow, they didn't have any children. Year after year went by, and each year the

Tortoises hoped that this would be the year that they would have young.

Finally, the husband Tortoise went to the Creator, and humbly asked if their greatest wish could be granted. Their long, long years together, he said, had been empty without any young of their own.

The Creator told Tortoise that he and his wife were, by then, too old to have children. Tortoise's wife would surely die from the strain, He said. The Tortoises must be content with each other's companionship.

Tortoise and his wife were greatly disappointed. After a while, Tortoise thought to himself, "Surely the Great One is mistaken. If we do not have young ones, who will follow us? And like the rocks we resemble, surely we must be ageless." So back he went to the Creator. But his plea was met with the same reply.

Now Tortoise really was convinced that the Creator must be wrong. Finally he threw himself at the Great One's feet, for the third and last time.

The Creator was moved at Tortoise's courage, persistence and sorrow, so He let the couple have their young ones.

He also gave Tortoise the following advice: "Tell your wife to take very good care of herself. She is really much too old to produce eggs. But when her time comes for egg-laying, she must watch the eggs carefully. She must

keep them warm, but not let them get too hot. She must protect them with her body until they hatch."

Old Tortoise was overjoyed, and rushed home with the good news. But he did not mention that the strain might kill his wife. He instructed her on the care of her eggs, and she carefully followed the advice of the Creator. She ate well, took care to rest a lot, and did no heavy work.

She managed to lay the eggs without too much trouble, and after the incubation time was over, and four lovely baby tortoises were hatched, she looked after them just as the Creator had advised.

However, as in all matters, the Great One was right. The old mother tortoise, taxed beyond her strength, died. The bereaved husband did his best to care for his young ones, but soon he too died, of a broken heart.

The Great One looked down with pity upon the orphaned babies, and decided to care for them Himself. He guided each to food, and provided for them.

And now, no mother tortoise ever has to care for her eggs, or her babies; for the Creator ordered the Sun to warm the eggs, and when tortoise babies are hatched, each one is able to take care of itself. The Creator shows it where to find food, and how to hide inside its shell when danger threatens.

FACTS ABOUT TORTOISES
SPECIES:
HINGED TORTOISE *(Kinixys bellania bellania)*
Solitary.

	Male	Female
Length	8 in	8¾ in
Weight	3⅓ lb	4½ lb
Length at Hatching	1½ in	1½ in
Age at Maturity	8 years	8 years
Incubation Period	12 months	12 months
Number of Eggs	—	2 or 3
Lifespan	20 years	20 years

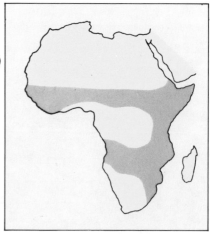

Identification The tortoise is a relative of the turtle. Both have a body encased in a shell of bone covered by horny shields. They can retract the head, limbs and tail inside this shell. There are no teeth in the jaw, which instead has a horny cutting edge.

Habitat Southern Africa possesses a great many species of tortoise, living in many different environments. Some live in the water and are known as terrapins. Southern Africa hosts the world's greatest variety of land tortoises.

Habits During winter most tortoises hibernate in snug-fitting holes which they dig in old termite mounds or banks of earth. There they stay until the first rains of summer, when they wake up. Their worst enemy is the bush fire, because they move too slowly to get out of the way. They are also prey for many predators; including eagles, which have learned to drop them from a height in order to break the shell.

Diet Tortoises are vegetarian, eating most kinds of grass, succulent plants, fungi and fallen fruit. They have been seen gnawing at old bones, probably to obtain minerals and sharpen the jaw rather than as food.

Breeding They mate when the first rains come and the female lays six to 12 eggs in a hole that she has dug. The hole is then covered over and smoothed down. The young, which hatch in the next rainy season, are born complete with a shell and are ready to fend for themselves immediately.

GLOSSARY

Baobab
A tree widely distributed throughout the drier, low-lying areas of Africa. These long-lived trees are distinctive because of their huge girth, smooth bark and cream-of-tartar seed pods.

Browser
An animal that eats mainly from trees and shrubs, taking leaves, twigs and shoots, rather than grazing or eating grass.

Bush
A general term applied to areas in southern Africa that still resemble the natural or original state.

Calabash
See Gourd.

Carnivore
An animal that lives by eating other animals.

Diurnal
Term describing an animal that is active during the hours of daylight. (*See also* Nocturnal.)

Ecology
The study of the relationship between living things and their environment, including both their non-living surroundings and other animals.

Endangered
A term applied to an animal that is threatened with extinction, usually due to pressure from mankind either directly (from over-hunting and poaching) or indirectly (by changing the creature's habitat). The World Wildlife Fund's "Red List" is a list of the animals most threatened with extinction.

Extinction
When a species no longer exists either in the wild or in captivity it is said to be extinct. Extinction is forever!

Gemsbok cucumber
The fruit of a creeping plant, common in many dry areas. This fruit, although bitter, contains a lot of moisture and is important to man and wildlife in the dry season.

Gestation Period
The period of time required for a mammal to develop in its mother's womb from the date of conception through to birth.

Gourd
The dried and hollowed-out shell of a fruit related to the melon. In Africa gourds are widely used as water containers and drinking vessels.

Grazer   An animal that feeds on grass.

Gregarious   A gregarious animal is one that lives in flocks or herds.

Habitat   The immediate surroundings of a creature or plant, that normally provide everything it requires to live.

Herbivore   An animal that feeds on plants.

Heritage   Our natural heritage is the natural environment left to us by our ancestors and which we are entrusted to hand on to future generations.

Hibernate   A creature hibernates when it spends time in a deep sleep or torpor to avoid harsh climatic conditions such as cold winters.

Honey-guide   A small brown bird that eats insect larvae and grubs. It has the peculiar habit of guiding man and honey-badgers to beehives in the bush. It then eats the leftovers.

Hunter-gatherer A term applied to nomadic tribes such as the Bushmen of southern Africa who live off the land rather than relying on crops and livestock.

Incubation period The period of time required for a bird or reptile to develop in its egg from the time the egg is laid until the day it hatches.

Inganga   A southern African name for a witch doctor.

Kopje   An Afrikaans name used throughout southern Africa to describe a small rocky hill or outcrop.

Kraal   Either an area protected by a stockade or fence, for containing livestock; or a village.

Leguaan   *See* Water-monitor.

Mammals   A term for the group of animals that are warm-blooded, have milk-producing glands, are partly covered in hair and normally bear their young alive. This group includes man, elephant, baboon and bats.

Migrate

Animals migrate when they undertake seasonal movements, often covering long distances, because of variations in food or water supplies due to changing seasons.

Muti

A southern African term for traditional medicines.

Nocturnal

A nocturnal creature is one that is active by night. (*See also* Diurnal.)

Omnivore

A creature that eats both meat and vegetation.

Oxpecker

A small African bird closely related to the starling. It is so named because it sits on the backs of cattle and eats ticks and other insects.

Pan

A natural waterhole.

Predator

An animal that catches other animals for food.

Prey

Any animal caught by a predator.

Pride

A family group of lions.

Resource

Something available as a stock or reserve that can be used when needed.

Reptile

A cold-blooded animal with scaly skin, e.g. snakes and lizards.

Sanctuary

A safe place, such as a national park, where animals are usually free from threat.

Savannah

Extensive areas of natural grassland.

Scavenger

An animal that lives off the dead remains of other animals or plants, e.g. jackals and vultures, which scavenge from the remains of lion kills.

Solitary

A solitary animal is one that lives alone, without companions for most of the time.

Species

A term, singular or plural, for a group of animals or plants with common characteristics and which do not breed with others.

Territory　　　　　An area used by an animal for feeding and/or breeding, often defended against its own kind and sometimes against other species too.

Tsamma melon　　　A creeping plant found in dry areas. Its large fruit contain moist, pulpy seeds and are an important food source to man and wildlife in the dry season.

Umbrella tree　　　A large, flat-topped acacia common in many areas of Africa.

Veld　　　　　　　*See* Bush.

Vlei　　　　　　　An Afrikaans name widely used in southern Africa for an area of marshy ground.

Wallow　　　　　　A mud- or dust-bath in which animals lie and roll to cool off and obtain protection from skin parasites such as ticks and lice.

Water-monitor　　　A large lizard, growing up to 6¾ ft (2 m) long, common throughout most of Africa and closely associated with rivers and dams.

Weaning　　　　　The stage at which a young animal is no longer dependent on its mother's milk and starts to eat the same food as the adult.

BIBLIOGRAPHY

AFRICAN MYTHS AND LEGENDS. Kathleen Arnott, Oxford University Press, 1962
ANIMALS OF RHODESIA. Astley Maberly, Howard Timmins, 1963.
BANTU FOLKLORE. Matthew L. Hewat, M.D., T. Maskew Miller, 1906
BIRDS OF SOUTH AFRICA. Austin Roberts, The Trustees of the John Voelker Bird Book Fund. Distributed by C. Struik, 4th ed., 2nd imp., 1978
COMMON SNAKES OF SOUTH AFRICA. John Visser, Purnell & Sons, 1979
FIELD GUIDE TO THE LARGER MAMMALS OF AFRICA. Jean Dorst and Pierre Dandelot, Collins, 2nd ed., 1972
LEGENDARY AFRICA. Sue Fox, Everton Offset, 1977
MAMMALS OF THE KRUGER AND OTHER NATIONAL PARKS. H. Kumpf; a publication of the National Parks Board of Trustees of the Republic of South Africa.
MATABELE FIRESIDE TALES. Phyllis Savory, Howard Timmins, 1962
MYTHS AND LEGENDS OF SOUTHERN AFRICA. Penny Miller, T.V. Bulpin, 1979
SIGNS OF THE WILD. Clive Walker, Natural History Publications, 1981
SOUTH AFRICAN FOLK TALES. James A. Honey, M.D., Baker & Taylor, 1960
SPECIMENS OF BUSHMAN FOLKLORE. W.H.I. Bleek and L.C. Lloyd, C. Struik, 1968
SWAZI FIRESIDE TALES. Phyllis Savory, Howard Timmins, 1973
TALES FROM THE OKAVANGO. Thomas J. Larson, Howard Timmins, 1972
THE BIRDS OF AFRICA. Vol. I, Leslie Brown, Emil Urban and Kenneth Newman, Academic Press, 1982
THE BUSHMAN SPEAKS. Mary Philips, Howard Timmins, 1961
THE GAME ANIMALS OF SOUTHERN AFRICA. C.T. Astley Maberly, Nelson, 1963
THE MAMMALS OF RHODESIA, ZAMBIA AND MALAWI. Reay H.N. Smithers and E.J. Bierley, Collins, 1966.
THE MAMMALS OF THE SOUTHERN AFRICAN SUBREGION. Reay H.N. Smithers, University of Pretoria, 1983
XHOSA FIRESIDE TALES. Phyllis Savory, Howard Timmins, 1963
ZULU FIRESIDE TALES. Phyllis Savory, Howard Timmins, 1961